HILDEGARD GÜNZEL

Creating Original Porcelain Dolls

Modeling, Molding, And Painting

Published by Hobby House Press

Grantsville,
Maryland 21536

This book is dedicated to my girlfriend, Astry Campbell.

Acknowledgments

I would like to thank all who supported me with my artistic development and the preparation and realization of this book. I would like to especially thank my family for having so much understanding and patience.

I had a lot of fun working with my niece, Antje Günzel, who was decisively responsible for the text of this book. My niece, Andrea Gehrig, helped me during the development of this book by endeavoring to take care of all my business things. Mathias Wanke supported me through his trust in my work and his solidarity.

Had Bruno Kapahnke not existed, I would never have had so much excellent photographic material to fall back on. I also would like to thank Astry Campbell, who in the last few years was a kind-hearted consulting girlfriend.

Maria Gentner, my seamstress, I have to thank for the realization of all the wonderful and exquisite doll clothes.
Eckhard Rasch (died 1987) and Michael Wanke advised me patiently with the technical problems.

Thanks to all my colleagues in the doll studio for all of their kind-hearted help and favors, especially when I thought that my work was going to go over my head.

Finally, I would like to give my special thanks to the one person who, when I was still a little child, always believed in my artistic talent, my mother. She made it possible with a lot of foregoing by financing my studies as a designer in Munich at the German Master School of Fashion.

She thereby laid, maybe unwillingly, the foundation for my success as a doll artist.

Hildegard Günzel

To page 2: All-porcelain body doll — 30½in (80cm).

Table of Contents

© 1987 by Verlag laterna magica,
    München
Federal Republic of Germany
All rights reserved

Copyright of the English language
    edition
© 1988 by Hobby House Press, Inc.,
    Grantsville, Maryland
United States of America
3rd printing, 1994

Translation: Michael T. Robertson

Text and Text Revision: Antje Günzel and Hildegard Günzel

Photographs: Foto-Studio Bruno Kapahnke, Schömberg

Page 109 below and page 110: Eduard Noak

Technical Advisors: Eckhard Rasch (died 1987), Michael Wanke, Mathias Wanke, Maria Gentner

References: *German Doll Encyclopedia* by Jürgen & Marianne Cieslik, Otto Mayer Verlag, Ravensburg

ISBN: 0-87588-339-7
Printed in Germany

D.L. B 27720-88

Introduction

With this book *Creating Original Porcelain Dolls,* Verlag Laterna Magica and Hobby House Press create new accents in the framework of their well-known literature. The creative hobby of making ones own doll has in the last few years spread like wildfire and for this particular group of admirers, a large need exists for information. This had already been recognized for years by competent insiders. For example, in 1980 Mathias Wanke had already occupied himself with this topic and he started the ball rolling. He organized doll courses and engaged for this an internationally well-known expert, Astry Campbell, from America to conduct these courses. She wrote the following:

"In June of 1984 the first course was started in Limburg, and ten young talented women applied to take part. From my many years of experience, I developed a course which made it easier for every participant to gradually step into the art of sculpting."

Highly talented and successful artist doll makers like, for example, Rotraut Schrott, Carin Lossnitzer, Rosi Panskus and, of course, the author, Hildegard Günzel, profited from her treasures of experience and knowledge, which she unselfishly passed on.

The vanguard of former times and several other great talents today influence the international creativily of artist dolls. Hildegard Günzel interprets in didactically perfect preparation, with the assistance of Antje Günzel and the photographer, Bruno Kapahnke, the self making of artist dolls in word and picture in a step by step technique, starting from the modeling of the heads, hands and feet and ending with the dressing of the dolls. Naturally, the "participant in the course" is also introduced to the knowledge of material and equipment, so that optimal results are obtained. Precisely within this area, Mathias Wanke, who has already been mentioned, and his company deserve to be merited, because he was the one who tested which material and equipment was best suited for the making of ones own artist doll, which he then offered for the practical use for sale.

The author, Hildegard Günzel, is an artist whose dolls are highly coveted by collectors. She is also a competent teacher who holds doll classes. She has been honored with prizes and awards and is presented with her own doll creations at all major doll conventions and competitive shows throughout the world.

With *Creating Original Porcelain Dolls,* a do-it-yourself book is offered to those who are interested, and who will never dispense with it. This book wants to encourage the making of dolls — an independent hobby, which guarantees to everyone talent, self-realization and success.

Joachim F. Richter, Publisher

◀ *Bajazzo* with mask from the group *Comedia dell 'Arte,* 30½in (80cm), White porcelain with costume of painted silk painted silk painted fabric.

The Development of Artist Dolls

The large world of dolls, which does not only exist of fantasy of lace, velvet and silk, but also shows historical, social and artistic background, exists in reality. Its modern story begins in the 19th century, where the German doll industry experienced its first climax. At the beginning of the 20th century, the term "Artist Doll" was introduced, which in contrast to the actual play doll, found more usage as a superior term for a completely different type of doll.

The reason for this came from an idea of a departmental head for toys from the department store Tietz in Munich. With the aim to increase the demand for dolls and with new ideas, boost the interests of the buyers in this business, he summoned the various artists to produce their own dolls for an exhibition.

Doll Exhibitions

The only requirement was that the dolls should be child-like. Many artists whose names today are still not forgotten participated at this exhibition. For example, Marion Kaulitz, next to the others, took over the control of the exhibition. The dolls which were exhibited here caused an unusual sensation since they were not dull and boring factory goods, but small persons — playmates for the children. That was in the year 1908 in Munich. One year later in Berlin, also at the department store Tietz, a doll exhibition took place which had the exact similar reform thoughts which Max Schreiber, the departmental head in Munich, initiated. In Berlin one artist took part, introducing her dolls to the critics and buyers great success. After nearly 80 years, her name is still on all tongues — Käthe Kruse.

Her ideal conception came far closer to the play doll for children than the models of the other artists, since one could dress and undress her dolls, wash their faces and their bodies and her dolls were soft and cuddly.

Most of the artist dolls of that time distinguished themselves from the others because they wore precious clothing and were more often than not objects for display cases or for sofa corners. The result was that they were not suitable for children to play with and due to this, they lost market value. Therefore, a lot of the doll artists could not extract any economical gain from their work and their lucky star fell as fast as it had risen.

At the same time as the doll reform, the creation of the first artist doll and the success of several artists such as Marion Kaulitz, Käthe Kruse and Lotte Pritzel, a new hobby was developed by the "ladies of

A dancer from the group *Comedia Dell'Arte*, 35³/₈in (90cm). Each hair in wig is separately knotted.

Amateur Dolls

Schildkröt

society." Encouraged by wide public interest, they tried to produce their own dolls. The reason that this hobby was especially for women in the middle class is quite obvious. Only they had the necessary financial means and time to keep themselves occupied by creating dolls. The dolls from these women were called "Amateur dolls."
This expression was coined by the press because they were not impressed by the activities of these women. Naturally, it is worth considering why such a shattering judgment had been made over these amateur dolls. Maybe they were afraid that these women would invade the men's territory, since the doll industry was without a doubt this. From the turn of the century onwards, it was mainly men who had come to terms with making and selling dolls. The designs also came from men, mainly sculptors. Art-interested women suddenly appeared in the middle of this scene. They embodied their own ideas and creativity into their dolls and also had the courage to introduce these dolls to the general public.

If one compares the situation of today with then, one can conclude that the women have greatly achieved setting their feet into this large doll world. What caused the women to create their own dolls and not give up? Most likely this phenomena has a lot of reasons. Due to both world wars, the doll industry perished. A lot of women and girls lost their highly loved doll children. The generation which grew up during or after World War II hardly had any dolls to play with. Far more important things had to be done. A country and the means of existence had to be built. Some mothers, who felt sorry for their children and who were creatively inclined, produced with primitive means dolls for their children. After the build-up and the beginning of the economic wonder, life found its normal routine and dolls held a renewed march into the playrooms. For example, Schildkröt dolls and for those who could afford them, the Käthe Kruse dolls began to appear.

About 16 years ago, beginning with the first flea market, Germany was seized by the world-wide nostalgic wave. All of a sudden a lot of women were confronted at the flea markets with their toy dolls, which had been lost during the war. They felt a wonderful mood returning them to their childhood days.

Many of these women wished to once again own such a doll. That was the beginning of doll collecting and the foundation of many important doll collections. It was soon apparent that the supply of old dolls at reasonable prices was smaller than the demand. An American idea found a lot of followers in Europe. As the first company in Europe. In

◀ Breast-plate doll *Alexandra, 33¹/₂in (85cm)*.

Germany Wanke developed molds of old dolls so that doll collectors in reproduction classes had the possibility of resurrection an original copy of their missing, lost or burnt doll child. Nearly parallel to this, an artistic doll movement was created. Here women could freely model their own ideas and create a fantasy doll, in whose face and form was a reflection of their own desires and dreams. What these "new" doll artists undertook to do was not an easy task. They realized after a short time how many doubts and disappointments were involved with this act of realization. However, they had, even if it had taken a few years of hard work, learned with pain, sweat and tears the joys which were offered when a piece of artwork had been finished. They had invested a great deal of their own strength and time and this was reflected in their dolls. Pleased by these successful experiences, more and more women became interested in doll making. In the last few years in Germany and neighboring countries, courses, shows, fairs, conventions, exhibitions, slide-lectures, and so forth, were being held, where doll artists reported about their work, problems, success and experiences.

Reproduction Courses

Conventions, Fairs

In the long years of my work, which was not only of success, but also accompanied by hard work, I have been able to collect a lot of experience, a lot of lectures have originated from my work and a lot of photographs have been taken which document my work. I decided to collect all the documents together and use them as a basis for this book. The most important requirement for making dolls is the technique. Creativity and ideas alone are not enough. One needs to have the ability to transform them into a doll. Technique alone does not help either. Doll making is a type of self-experience.

Artist dolls are creations of fantasy, produced with sadness or joy, never for material reasons. If one makes a doll for motives of self-interest, it will never have a "soul" or expression, which actually is the aim of every doll artist.

Artists to produce dolls which are the mirror of their souls. A doll produced with this intention is never a cold and lifeless object. It may show mistakes and defects in proportion and workmanship, but it "lives."

If one looks at the development of the dolls in the last 90 to 100 years, an interesting development is shown. From a doll as a pure toy for children to an artist doll as a result of the reform movement, adjusted to the interests of art loving grown-ups, it developed finally into a serial produced and conceived artist doll for children as a toy. It was not only the doll industry which sold these artist dolls in series.

Doll Industry

Porcelain breast plate doll *Yüksell* with freely molded on, drenched in plaster silk. ▶

Several artists managed to set up their own production and sell partly world wide their own series of dolls.

Since the turn of the century, the development of artist dolls has made great progress, but I would like to go on one step further. It is definitely no utopia to work towards the future; the profession of a doll artist, similar to that in Czechoslovakia should be taken up in Germany as a qualified profession at arts and crafts schools. To those doll artists who see problems in this and who are afraid to pass on their tips, tricks and techniques, I would like to pass on a few words of a befriended and well-known doll artist: "Techniques can be learned, taught and also knowingly copied." The art which makes a "doll live" results from the talent of individual artists and can be copied but it will never have perfection.

Doll Artists

◄ *Colombine* from the group *Commedia dell 'Arte* — limited edition — 40in (100cm). Hand-painted silk dress.

Chapter 1

Anatomy and Theory of Proportions

At the beginning of every artist's development, a natural born talent exists. This talent is often the release mechanism for this interest, which, already in younger years, comes to be partially expressed. The same thing is the case with doll artists. They feel the urge to produce their own doll and with this attempt, they realize rather quickly when they have reached their artistic boundaries. Every type of art, may it be acting, literature or fashion, needs a basic amount of knowledge. With doll making it is, among other things, the knowledge about proportions. A doll artist must, to create in looks a harmonious figure, model the limbs and head as such so that when they are put together, the proportions are correct. That means:

Proportions

— The size of hands and feet must be in proportion to the head.

— The same thing applies for the arm and leg lengths.

Doll Bodies

— The doll body must be cut as such, that it resembles in proportion and mobility that of a human body.

To make dolls with the correct proportions, one must acquire the skill of modelling in nude or portrait classes, or if one is so talented, one can learn through self-teaching. It is, therefore, important to constantly observe ones fellow men. Every artist must train his eyes. The best model for an artist is a living object. Body posture, bearing of the hands, the position of the head, all these can be seen in various forms in people. Those who pay close attention will notice how different the proportions are with infants, small children, school children, youths and adults. Also, the body structure of women differs, besides the known sex characteristics, more than that of men. Here are differences which the layman overlooks. For example, the navel of a woman lies higher than that of man, or the pit of the stomach, which lies lower with women than with men and also one suspects that women have longer toros, which is not correct. If one looks at these examples of which I could quote still many more, it is rather advisable to have some training or at least detailed pursuit with the topic "proportions."

Body Structure

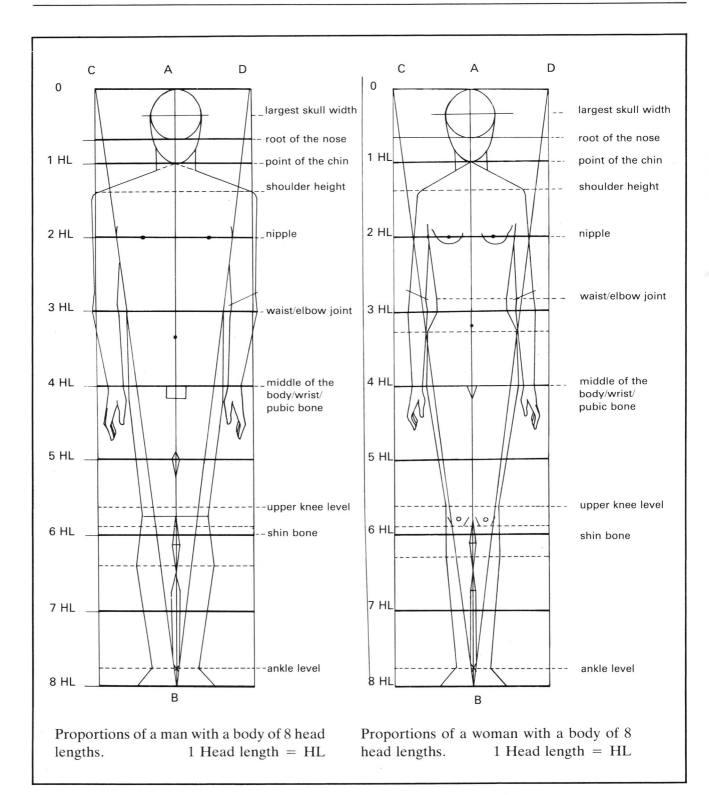

Proportions of a man with a body of 8 head lengths.   1 Head length = HL

Proportions of a woman with a body of 8 head lengths.   1 Head length = HL

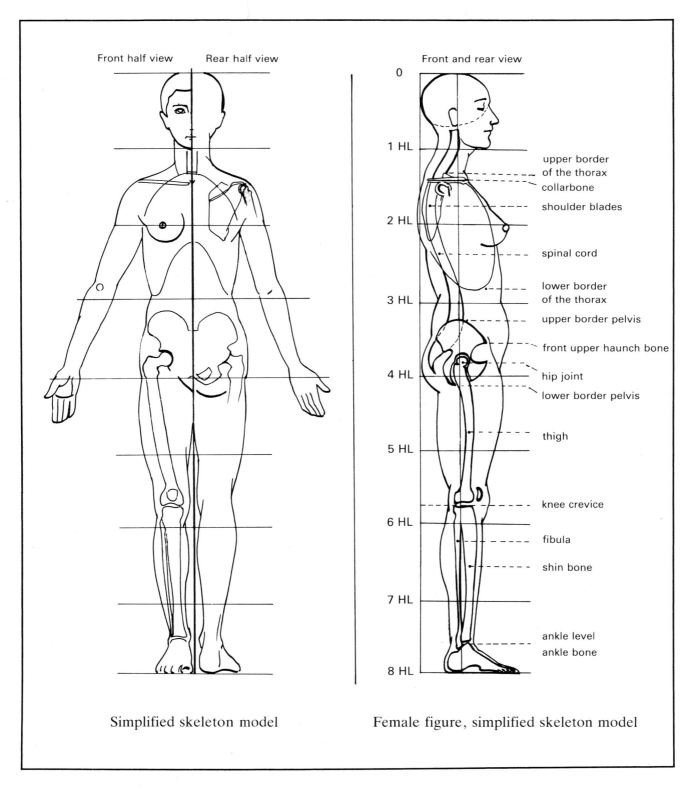

Front half view   Rear half view

Front and rear view

0

1 HL

upper border
of the thorax
collarbone

shoulder blades

2 HL

spinal cord

lower border
of the thorax

3 HL

upper border pelvis

front upper haunch bone

hip joint

4 HL

lower border pelvis

thigh

5 HL

knee crevice

6 HL

fibula

shin bone

7 HL

ankle level
ankle bone

8 HL

Simplified skeleton model

Female figure, simplified skeleton model

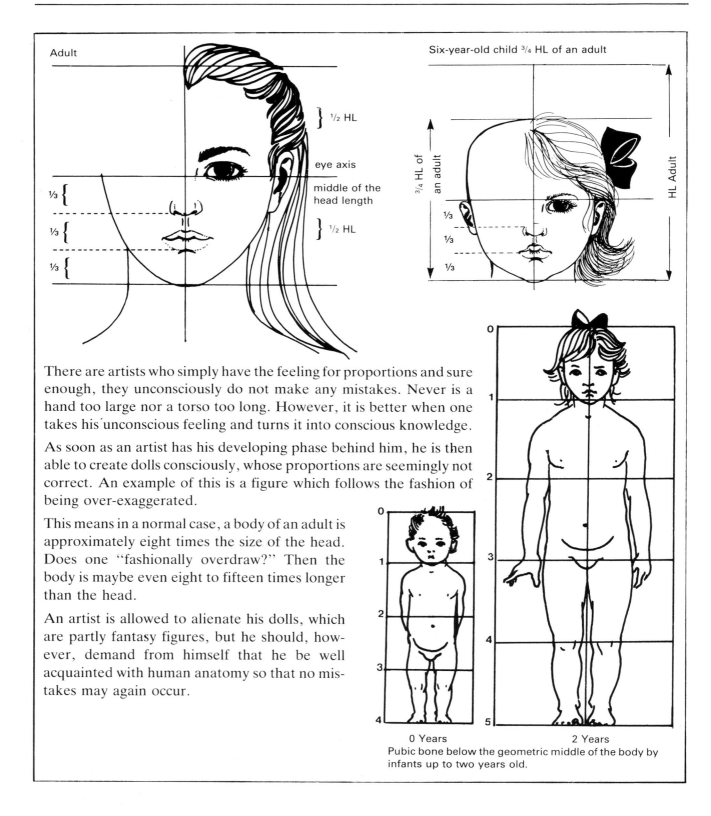

Adult

1/2 HL

eye axis

middle of the head length

1/3

1/3

1/2 HL

1/3

Six-year-old child 3/4 HL of an adult

3/4 HL of an adult

HL Adult

1/3

1/3

1/3

There are artists who simply have the feeling for proportions and sure enough, they unconsciously do not make any mistakes. Never is a hand too large nor a torso too long. However, it is better when one takes his unconscious feeling and turns it into conscious knowledge.

As soon as an artist has his developing phase behind him, he is then able to create dolls consciously, whose proportions are seemingly not correct. An example of this is a figure which follows the fashion of being over-exaggerated.

This means in a normal case, a body of an adult is approximately eight times the size of the head. Does one "fashionally overdraw?" Then the body is maybe even eight to fifteen times longer than the head.

An artist is allowed to alienate his dolls, which are partly fantasy figures, but he should, however, demand from himself that he be well acquainted with human anatomy so that no mistakes may again occur.

0 Years

2 Years

Pubic bone below the geometric middle of the body by infants up to two years old.

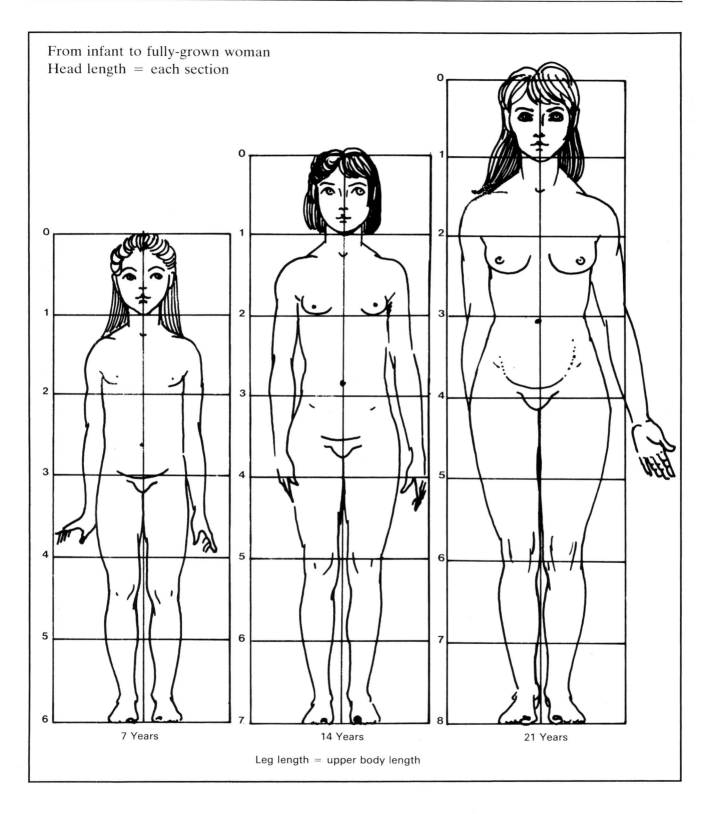

From infant to fully-grown woman
Head length = each section

7 Years

14 Years

21 Years

Leg length = upper body length

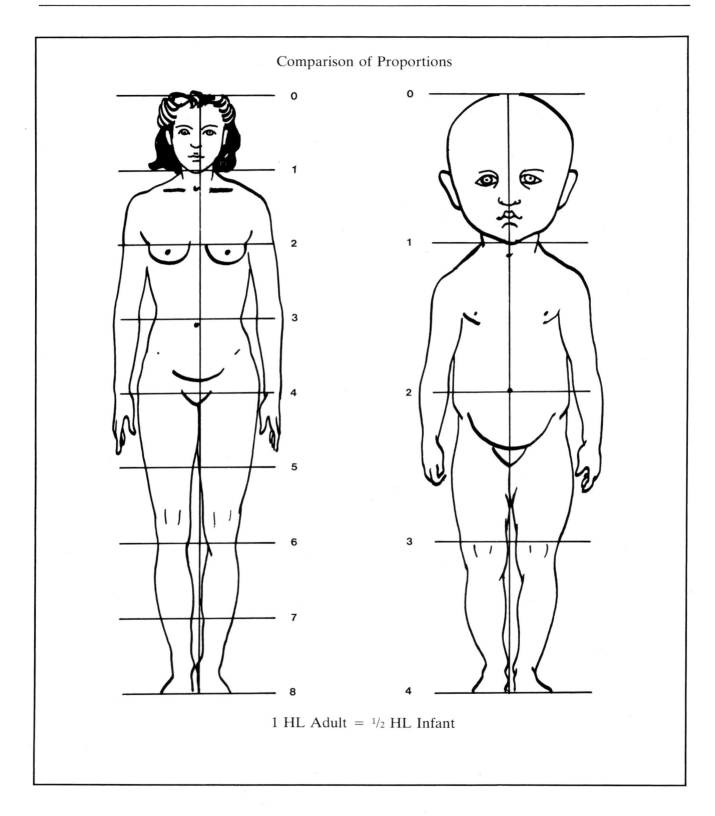

Comparison of Proportions

1 HL Adult = ½ HL Infant

*Chapter 2*_____

Modelling

You will notice in this chapter that certain subjects sometimes overlap. It shows how close one producing process is intertwined with another and, therefore, it is inevitable that by the modelling, one is sometimes referring to the mold making.

Mold Building

The Doll Artist

To create ones own artist doll demands that an artist be "a factory-in-one person." Besides artistic talent, he must also have a talent for handicrafts.

Doll Body

To design a doll, one must first draw a sketch, then model a doll and finally build a mold. Building a mold means proving ones own handicraftmanship. After the firing of the porcelain parts, these parts are then painted and finally they are connected with the doll body. Now begins the next creative phase. The doll artist must prove himself as a designer, who first designs the clothing for his doll and then tailors them. And to end all this, every artist should be a salesman because he must, if he wants to live from his occupation, be able to sell his works of art. It is rather rare that an artist, who lives in a fantasy world, is at the same time a good salesman. It would be ideal if one could aspire a balance between artistic and salesmanship talents. However, lately I have had this peculiar feeling that more and more women and men, who are swimming along with the "artist doll wave" put their emphasis more on salesmanship interests.

Try to make it a point to demand more and more skill from oneself. Forget the aspect of how well your doll can be sold. Dedicate your whole energy to the "high art" of doll making.

Modelling Material and Modelling Tools

For modelling you can choose from various materials. You can work with Cernit (modelling material with porcelain effect), clay, self-drying material or with an oil-based modelling material (Plastilin, Wankelin).

For a long time I have been modelling with "Wankelin" which is softer when warmed up and hardens when one places it into the

refrigerator. Wankelin can be used over and over again. If one works in various stages, one can observe that the newly applied Wankelin binds well with the old one.

Modelling Procedure

Since the most experience I have had was with using Wankelin, I will explain and demonstrate the modelling procedures with this material. To make the fine details of your Wankelin models, you need modelling tools which are either made of wood or metal and can be bought at a hobby shop.

Dental tools are also excellent for use in modelling. A famous doll maker modelled her beautiful dolls with a coffee spoon. You can improvise and use, for example, manicure instruments — use whatever comes to mind! What you really do need to buy for modelling is a

Modelling Wheel

modelling wheel which enables you to view the head from all sides and to recognize immediately your mistakes so that you can correct them.

Also very helpful for modelling is an external calliper which is useful in measuring eye distance and with which you can determine the other proportions on the head. Such a calliper can be purchased in a hobby shop.

Polaroid Camera

A polaroid camera can also be useful when modelling. With it you can capture your doll head in each stage of development.

This is very important because on a two-dimensional photograph, many anatomical mistakes which occur during the modelling can be

Three-dimensional Doll Head

seen far more clearly than with a three-dimensional head.

Should you have problems removing the head from the modelling wheel after the completion of the modelling process, then you should use a modelling sling. This sling has two wooden blocks which are connected by a strong wire or a sturdy nylon thread.

Lay this wire around your model, cross the ends of the wooden blocks and then pull apart forcefully.

◀ Socket head doll - breast plate with molded-on arms.

Head and Limbs

An artist who wants to make a doll take shape will first of all let his fantasies loose on paper.

Design

Do the same thing. However, afterwards make another design where your fantasy, knowledge and talent are brought into unison. Always be aware that from your design on paper you later have to make a mold.

It is important to make a technical drawing of the finished doll because the individually assembled limbs, body and the head must form a unit after completion. It is, therefore, necessary that before you begin with the modelling, you should know what type of body posture the doll should have. The position of the feet and hands are dependent as a unit on the type of head and vice versa.

Types of Heads

Breast Plate

There are various types of doll heads, the flange neck head being the simplest. A little more difficult is the head with the molded-on breast plate. The third type of head is the socket head, which demands more of your capabilities. You model the head and breast plate separately and connect them once they are finished.

You also have a choice of various possibilities of modelling the limbs. You can model the arms and legs only to the elbow or knee and after firing and painting them, you can sew them onto a cloth or leather body. Or you can model them to include the elbow and knee joints.

The most difficult of all are the all-porcelain dolls, since here porcelain is connected to porcelain. You can see that your fantasy knows no boundaries, assuming that your technical knowledge keeps in step.

Let us now return to the body position of your doll. If your doll bears its foot like a dancer, then a flange neck head will not be suitable because it does not move. A socket head would be far more suitable because by bending or turning the head, it radiates something dynamic. You also have to plan when designing the arms and legs of your doll. Try to keep a complete picture in front of your eyes so that a harmonius whole is created.

In many years of work with my students, I have noticed that when modelling, beginners always make the same mistakes. At this point I would like to list them so that time and frustration are saved.

Become conscious that a modeller, just like a sculptor, works three-dimensionally! At the beginning, a mistake is often made when one

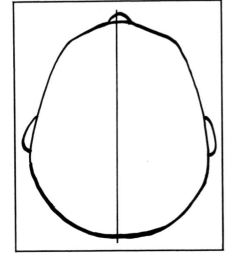

The skull from above. The back of the skull is wider.

draws, instead of modelling "freely." Train your eyes for the three-dimensional!

Start to understand that the oval of the skull becomes wider at the back of the head. The eyes do not lie on a two-dimensional horizontal line, but instead on an oval line! The result is that the inner angle of the eye lies higher than the outer one. The same thing applies for the corners of the mouth, which lie deeper on the oval line than the lips. (Examples for these are seen on antique sculptures.)

The ears lie lower on smaller children and are larger in comparison to adults.

Make sure that the ears are three-dimensional! A good doll maker is recognized by his modelled hands, feet and ears. Do not be satisfied with lovely shoes on bad feet or lovely wigs on bad ears! Try to always remember when modelling that the feet are always larger than the hands, and that a hand of a person is nearly large enough to cover the whole face. Beginners often underestimate the width of the neck. Look at the necks of infants and small children! You will see that small children hardly have any necks; the head seems to the observer to be practically resting on the shoulders.

The nose is very difficult to model. With nearly every head that one observes in profile, it will be noticed that the ridge between the nostrils lies deeper than the nose wings. Therefore, the nostrils are always seen in profile (see diagram).

The requirements for a lovely mold and a smooth porcelain head at the final stage are that your model head be very smooth and cleanly made. You can achieve this with Wankelin, by dipping your hands again and again into warm water or into talcum powder and rubbing them gently over the head.

It makes no difference how you do it. Both methods will make the head very smooth. When using talcum powder, the head obtains a wonderful silky sheen.

It is important that you like your doll at the beginning stages and that you build up a relationship with it. Try to make contact, even though you have only modelled the basic shape of the head and neck, by inserting the eyes into the doll's head. Now you can look at it, speak with it and it can ask you with its eyes, "Make something lovely out of me!"

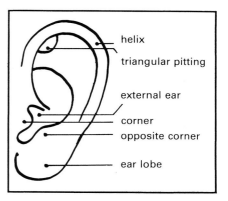

Anatomy of the ear.

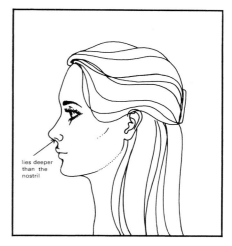

Side view of the head. Deeper lying nose ridge.

Undercuts

Later, you take apart the two plaster molds and lift the upper mold (face half) off vertically. To prevent any damage to the porcelain blank, there should not be any projections inside the mold half. If there are, the porcelain blank could get stuck and be damaged. It may even fall apart. In the technical language, one calls these projections "undercuts." Undercuts can occur through deep nostrils, modelled-out ears, an inclined chin or unprecise bedding of the model head.

The Modelling of a Flange Neck Head

The mother instincts of adults are simply aroused when they see chubby cheeks, the high-curved forehead, the overhanging upper lip and the large eyes. These characteristics fall under the main term "child pattern" in the technical language. This is what lets the adults break out in joyous raptures when they see these children. Pay attention to these when modelling your baby doll.

Child Pattern

On the following pages you will see the modelling of a small child. The characteristics of the child pattern are not so dominant as with a baby; however, they are clearly noticeable. The freckled-faced small child, *Guste*, is always good for surprises. It can be bought in special hobby shops as an artist doll mold.

Artist Doll Molds

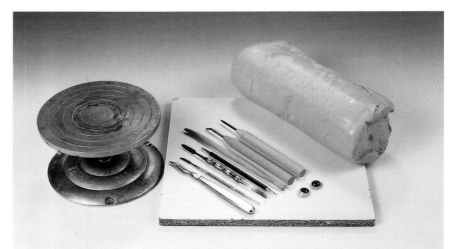

Materials: Modelling wheel - modelling tools - oil-based Wankelin - modelling material.

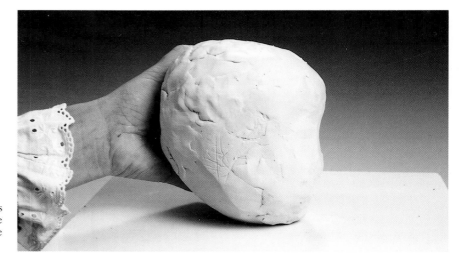

The skull is modelled first. The skull gets wider towards the back. Model the rear of the head and indicate a slight depth for the eye sockets.

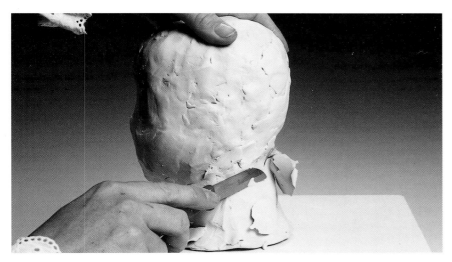

Add a piece of Wankelin for the neck. By cutting off the Wankelin around the neck, you can obtain the right width.

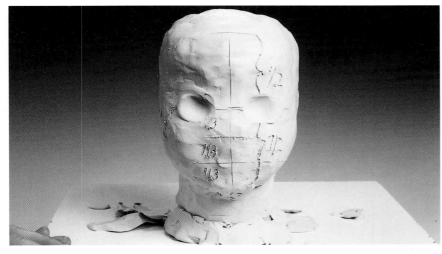

Now start with the division of the face. Divide the face into two halves and then take the lower half and divide it further into thirds.

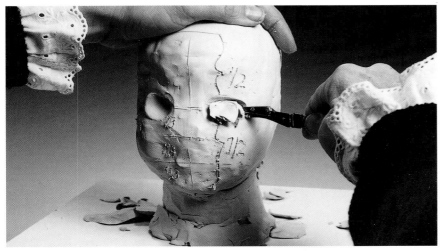

Cut out the eye sockets.

Insert the plastic eyes. Constantly check whether the head is anatomically correct from the side and rear.

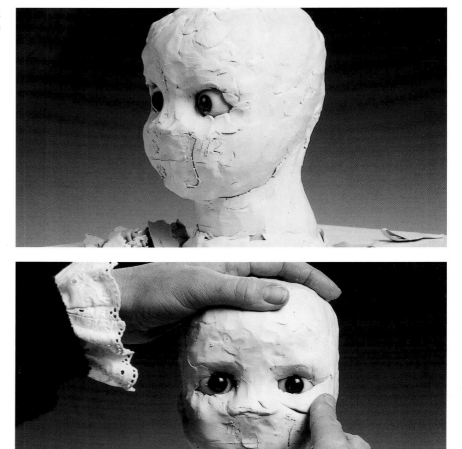

Model the lower lid. Make sure the outer angle of the eye lies lower than the inner one.

Model the nose, completing the nose wings, which as described before, lie higher than the nose ridge.

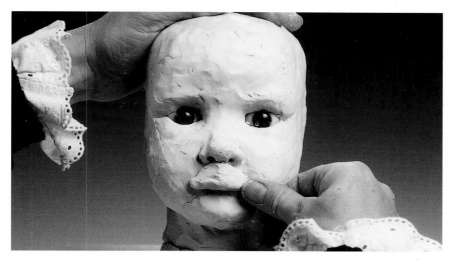

Roll the modelling clay and place it on as an upper lip.

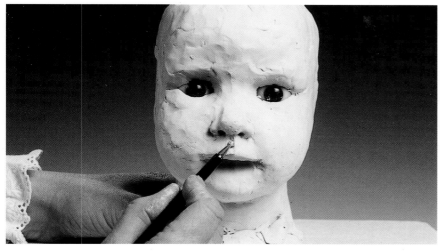

The upper lip is now modelled out; both of the lip curves go over into the nose furrow.

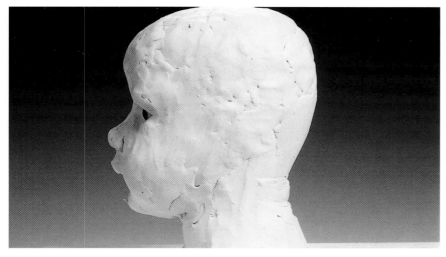

It is easier to model the chin before the lower lip. You can try both ways and determine which is the easiest for you and brings the best results. Model the shape of the chin and do not forget the dimple, above which the lower lip is placed.

Roll the modelling clay for the lower lip.

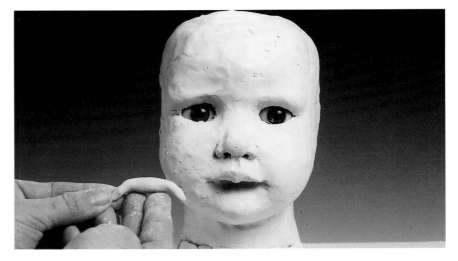

Apply the clay into position.

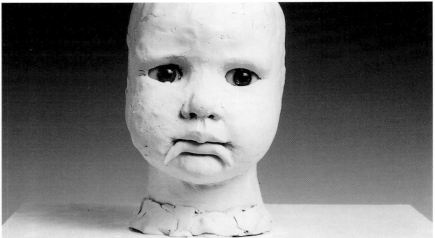

Always observe the head in profile.

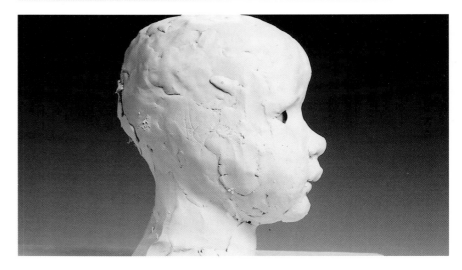

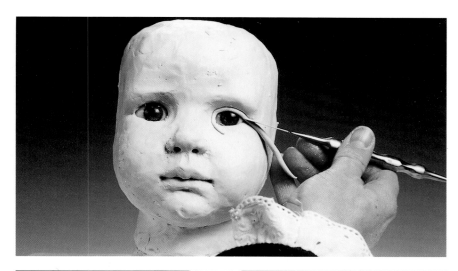

To model the upper eyelid, roll a piece of Wankelin until it is a fine strip. Make sure that the outer angle of the eye lies lower than the inner one. (See page 25.)

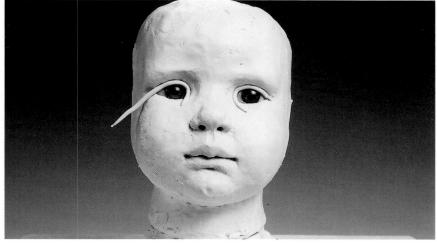

Fix the strip over the eye. Attach it using a modelling tool. Cut the remainder of the Wankelin off with a scalpel and begin the delicate modelling.

Make an indentation around the neck, which later is used for fastening.

To the illustrations on this page (top to bottom):

Draw the spot for the ears on the model head.

Roll a piece of Wankelin into a ball and divide it in half.

Both halves are modelled roughly into distinguishable ears and then attached to the head.

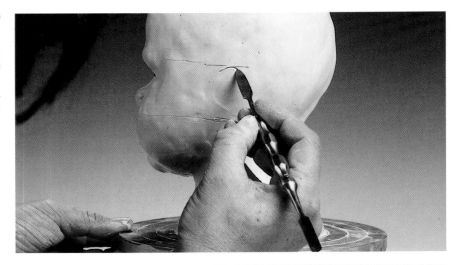

To the illustrations on page 33 (left side, top to bottom):

Correct the seating of the ears from behind. Do not forget to make the furrow in the nape of the neck, which merges with the spine.

Mark the positions of the ears where they have to sit with two toothpicks or with metal rods so that both ears are perfectly level.

Now you can begin the delicate modelling of the ears. Attach great importance to the anatomy.

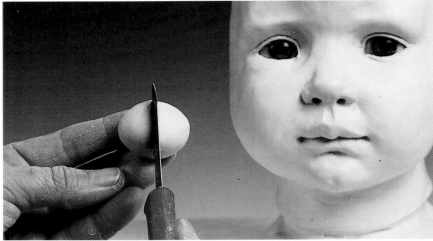

To the illustrations on page 33 (right side, top to bottom):

Observe that the ear is three-dimensional.

Rough modelling of the ear.

Finished ear. The external ear is cleanly worked out and very detailed.

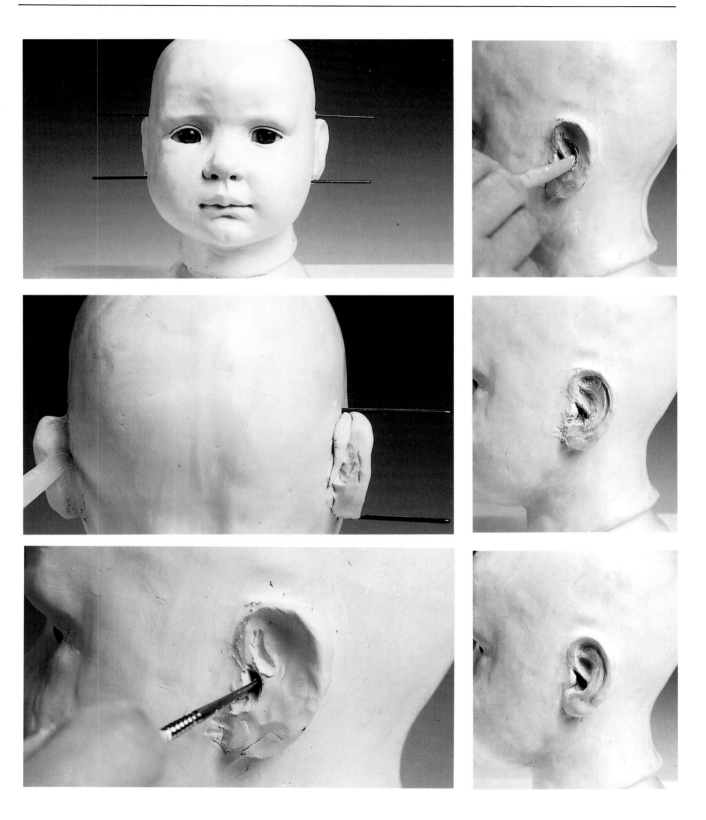

Completion of the modelling — head shown from the front, back and side view.

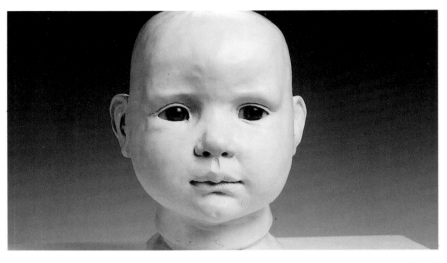

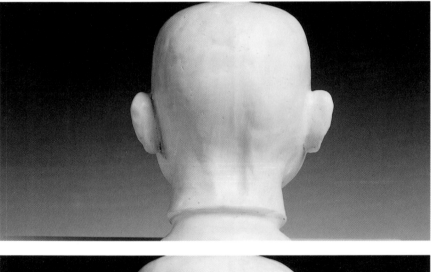

Photograph on page 35 ▶
Small child, *Guste* - flange neck head - the finished produced doll from the preceding model.

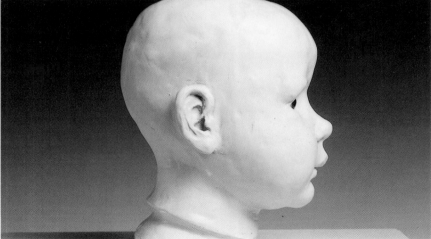

Head With Molded-On Breast Plate

Take a piece of laminated plywood and with the help of two diagonal lines, divide the board so that the middle point is found.

Above this point draw line for the back and below this point draw also a line for the chest. Both lines must be an equal distance from the middle point. The same thing is required for the left and right shoulder. The shoulders should have the same width and the neck with the head should be placed into the breast plate. That is why it is always recommended to make such a division on the work board for a model head with a molded-on breast plate.

Work Board

Draw the divisions on the laminated plywood.

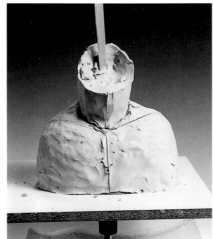
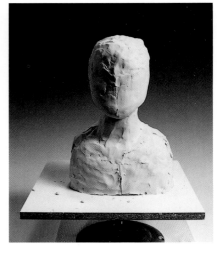

Model the chest, place the neck on and to increase the stability, model the head onto a piece of wood, which is then stuck through the neck and chest. ▶

Model the head and connect it to the neck and chest. ▶▶

Model out the shape of the skull.

Divide the face as described in the diagram of a woman's head shown on page 18. (Chapter on Anatomy and the Theory of Proportions). Always work the model head from all sides.

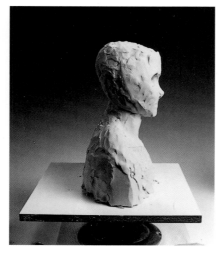

Model the collarbone and indicate the upper arms. Do not neglect the model head. As described already, work the head from all sides and make corrections, if necessary.

Press the eye sockets in and set the plastic eyes into the head. Model the nose, upper lip, chin and finally, the lower lip.

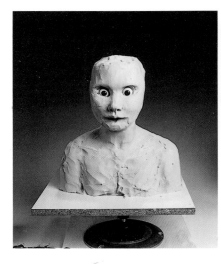 

The rough and delicate modelling of the face is now done in the same sequence as described with the flange neck head.

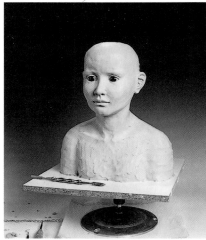 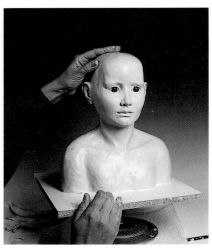

The ears can be modelled more deeply, since from this Wankelin model, a three-piece mold will be produced.

Do not forget the furrow in the back of the neck which runs from the back of the head into the neck and then goes over into the spine.

Finished example from the preceding photographs, *Fee*, limited edition, 40in (100cm), honored by the magazine *Dolls* during the 1987 New York Toy Fair with the "Award for Excellence." ▶▶

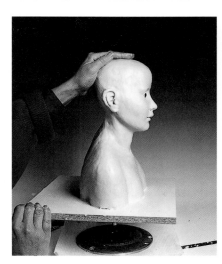 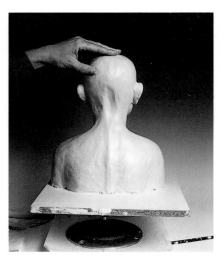

The Modelling of a Socket Head

To model a socket head, you use the same method which is used with the other model heads. You simply have to observe that the head does not end in a ring or that it has a molded-on breast plate, but that it ends with a rounded curve.

Neck

Breast Plate

Pouring Hole

To connect the neck to the breast plate wall, it is recommended that you use a styrofoam ball which can be bought in various sizes. In order that the curve ending of the neck fits into the opening of the breast plate, you have to cut a ball in half and use both halves as a mold. This has the advantage when producing various heads with the same size, the same breast plate can be used over and over again, saving you a lot of work and trouble. Have you directed your attention to the structure on top of the head? This is used after the mold is made for the pouring hole for the porcelain, completely opposite to the flange neck head, where the neck is used for the pouring hole.

Finished example from the preceding photographs, *Gabi*, limited edition, 40in (100cm).
▶

The breast plate is built up the same way as the molded-on breast plate; for this you need laminated plywood and the described divisions.

The neck opening is rounded off at the end of the modelling phase so that the positive rounding of the neck fits exactly into the negative half-ball of the neck opening.

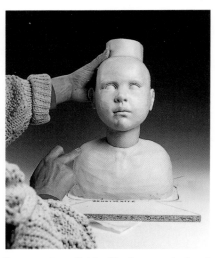

Once you have finished both parts, the head and breast plate, you must remember to place the structure of modelling clay on top of the head. This structure is used later as the pouring hole for the porcelain.

The Modelling of the Hands (with the example of the flange neck head)

The following illustrations show the modelling of the hands of a small child. To make it easier for you for the required mold making, the hands of a small child without the elbow and upper arm are modelled here. This type of modelling uses a two-piece mold. This does not mean that the hands have to be modelled without movement. You should bear in mind that the thumb is either pressed into the hand or pointing away; it should not be pointing inwards towards the palm of the hand. A strongly bent thumb or a half-opened fist have undercuts; this would require that the plaster mold would need more than two parts.

Place the head for which you want to model the arms and legs in front of you, enabling you to see whether the proportions of the limbs are in relationship to the head.

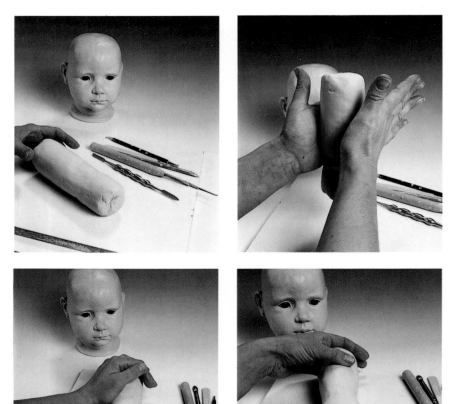

From a piece of Wankelin roughly model a wrist.

Widen out the end of the arm.

Make a cut for the thumb.

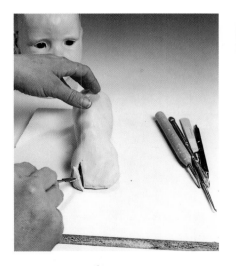

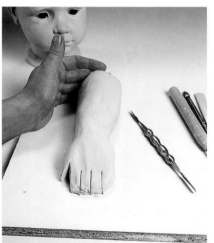

Produce a gap between the forefinger and thumb.

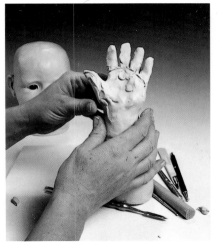

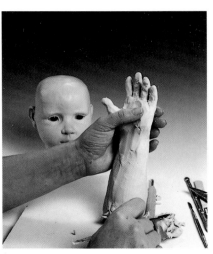

Very Important!
When the cuts are made for the other fingers, it is important to notice that they are not made as deep as the thumb. Round the fingers off at the tips. Stand the hand upright so that the palm of the hand is facing towards you. By comparing it with your hand, you will notice that the cuts made for the individual fingers run in an oval line from the forefinger towards the pinky finger.

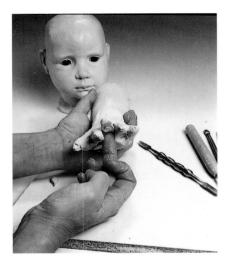

Press in the palm.

The small finger reaches right up to the last joint of the ring finger.

Make comparisons with your own hand.

With additional Wankelin you can now model the "Venus lump" (ball of the thumb).

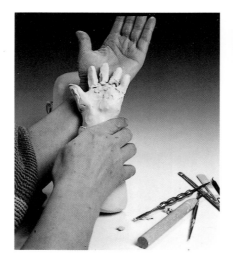 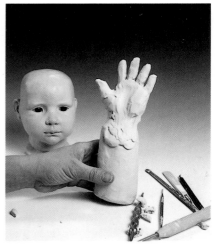

Remove any surplus Wankelin.

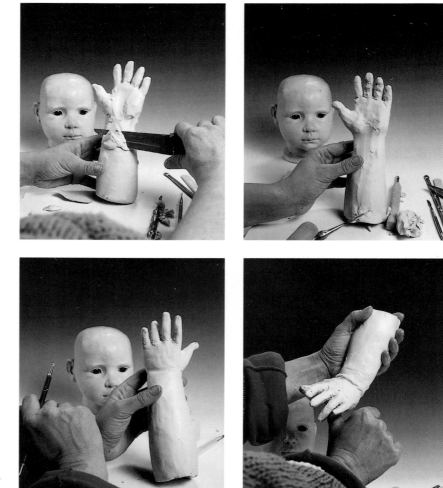

Now you can give your hand a graceful movement. Make sure that undercuts are avoided.

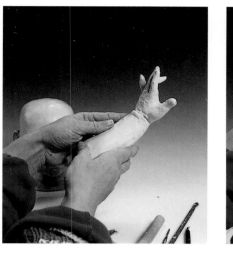

Start with the delicate modelling of the hands and stress the fatty layers on the wrist of the small child.

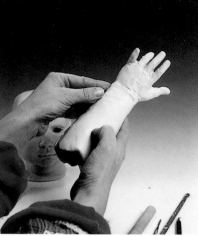

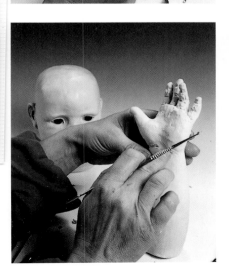

Correct the movement of the fingers. Draw lines on the fingers to show the separate joints. Work the back of the hand and the inner surface of the hand at the same time.

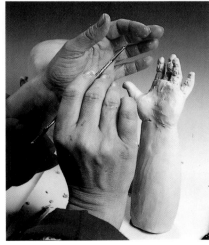

Work out the Venus hump in detail. Next model the finger joints. If no small child is available for comparisons, use your own hands.

45

Incise the lifeline.

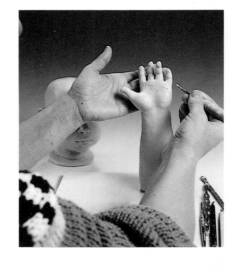

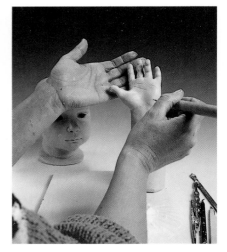

You can use your own hand as a comparison for helping you make the incisions. Rub the finished model hand smooth with talcum powder.

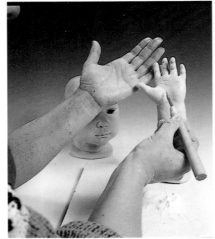

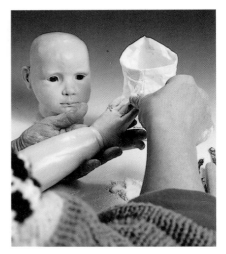

Check whether the proportions of the hand are in scale with the head. The smoother your work of the model is, the more exact your plaster mold will be later.

You now clearly see the differences between the hands of a small child and that of a young lady. The hands of an adult are more graceful, the fingers are longer, the wrists are narrower and the fatty layers have disappeared.

A detailed photograph of a finished porcelain hand of the model on page 49. ▶▶

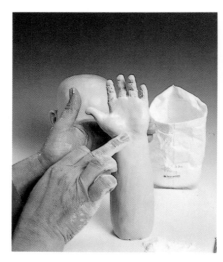

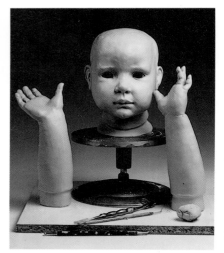

To the illustrations below:

Use your hand as the best example for modelling the hands of an adult.

You can see rather clearly that the hands of an adult are far more graceful and the fingers are longer, the wrist is narrower and the fatty layers have disappeared. ▶

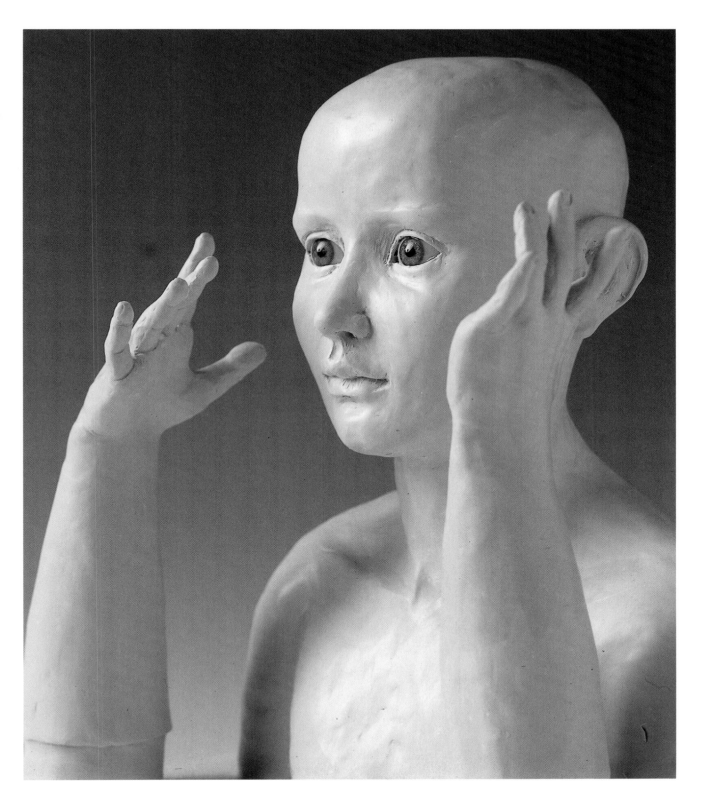

The Modelling of the Legs (with the example of the flange neck head)

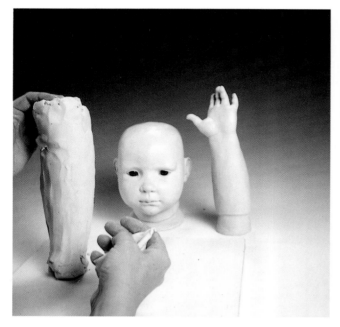

Always lay the head and arms next to you when modelling the leg so that the proportions can be compared.

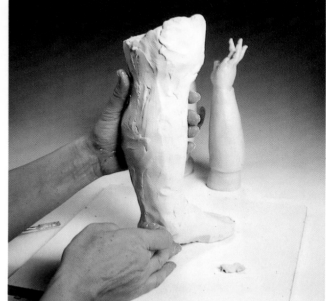

Roughly model the shape of the leg. Place the foot on.

Model the instep.

Model the sole of the foot. Do not forget the balls of the feet. Feet do not have flat soles!

Make the cuts for the toes.

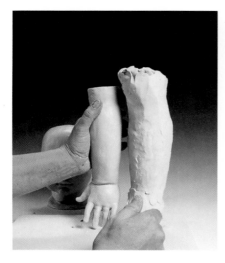

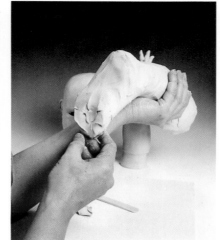

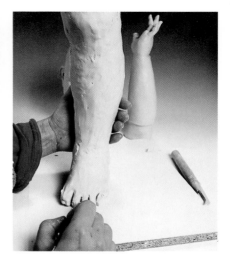

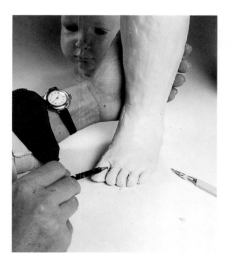

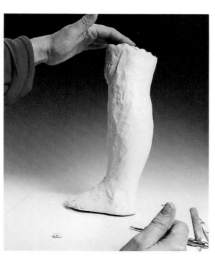

Model the toes.

Work out the details of the ankles. The inner ankle always lies higher than the outer ankle. This is clearly seen on page 52, upper left picture.

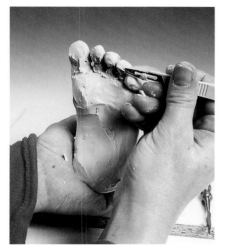

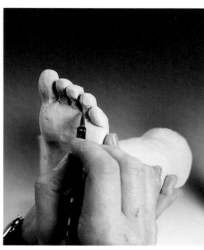

You now have to remove or add Wankelin to the toes. Carefully check that the cuts made for the toes are just like those for the hands. They run in a declining oval line from the large toe to small one. This oval line is much steeper than with the hand.

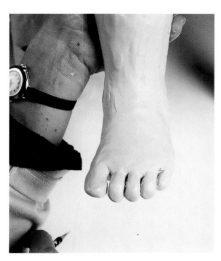

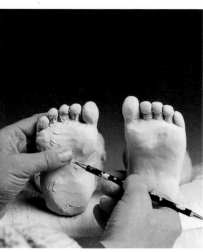

Draw the lines on the toes for the nails and model them. Smooth with talcum powder. Place the head and arm next to the leg for comparison.

For modelling the second leg, you can either use the same foot position as the first one or a different foot position. However, the size and length must be the same as the first foot.

Turn the leg again and again so that no mistakes are made. The knee, the bend of the knee and heels must be exactly worked out in detail. Smooth your model with talcum powder or water.

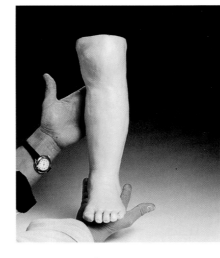

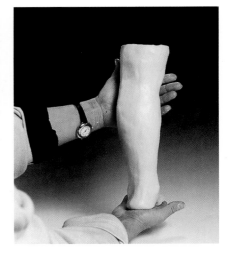

Lengthen the leg at the top because this opening will be used for pouring the porcelain into the hole.

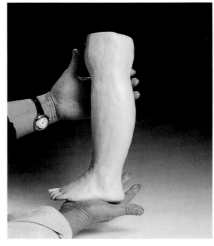

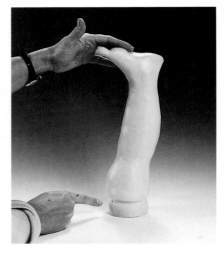

The completion of the modelling phase of both legs.

Place the head and limbs next to each other for comparing the proportions. If necessary, make corrections.

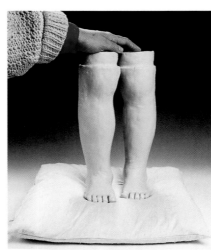

Resli, serial doll, three types of editions, 100 copies of each. Knees and thighs are molded on. ▶▶

List of materials needed for making the mold
of the flange neck head:
Laminated plywood board, Wankelin, angle
iron with mounted-on pencil, modelling rod,
tape, pane of plexiglass, long brush, spoon,
metal spatula, mold release fluid, mold plaster, hammer, rubber wedge, sharp knife.

*Chapter 3*_____

Mold Making

Difficulties are involved when working with plaster and I would like to reveal to you rules, tips and tricks so that you will not let yourself be outsmarted by this highly individual material.

Porcelain

There are many types of plaster but to produce molds, one needs to use a special molding plaster. Do not try to use normal plaster since it is not finely pored enough and it would leave behind an unevenness in the plaster mold and later on the porcelain head. You produce a negative copy with the plaster, which means that you make a mold of your Wankelin model and this mold is later filled with porcelain.

Basic Rules For Working With Plaster

There are several basic rules needed for working with plaster. Never pour water onto the plaster, but always the other way around. The warmer the water is into which the plaster is poured, the faster the plaster hardens. The colder the water is, the longer it takes for the plaster to harden. It is important to use an open bag of plaster rather

Humidity

quickly because plaster binds the humidity and, therefore, becomes unusable.

When plaster hardens or sets, a chemical reaction take place. The plaster begins to get hot. It takes between a half and one hour for the plaster to harden and cool down.

Finally, it is important to know that plaster is a very aggressive material and it should never, by any means, get into the eyes. If this does happen, rinse your eyes thoroughly with clear water. If you wish, you can protect your hands with thin rubber gloves.

Modelled Head

Finally, please note that plaster should never be poured into the It will harden in the drain pipes and you will need a plumber to repair it. Let the plaster harden in a plastic bucket and after it has hardened, dispose of it the garbage can. The smoother your model head is, the cleaner the mold will be and the less impurities and unevenness your porcelain head will have, thus requiring less sanding.

Sand Down Process

At the beginning it is very difficult to produce a clean first-class mold. This you can even out when doing the first sanding down process by taking warm water and a soft sponge, thus avoiding the development of porcelain dust.

Repairing Faulty Spots In The Plaster Mold

In the finished mold, when removing the Wankelin model, small holes may appear. These holes are created when the Wankelin head is covered with plaster and small air bubbles are trapped in the plaster. This damage can be repaired by taking a small plastic syringe, filling it with freshly stirred plaster or a paintbrush and then filling the holes up.

Mold Release

Plaster Block

If you want to produce a casting mold from a Wankelin model, be it the head, arm or leg, you must make sure when making the second part of the mold that the plaster of the existing mold half is painted with a light coat of mold release fluid! Wet plaster tends to bind with already hardened plaster. If your forget the mold release, your head may possibly remain stuck in the plaster mold. From my own experience, I can report that it is a nearly unsolvable undertaking for every "mother" to remove the head of the pitiful "child" from its plaster coffin. The doll will, before it is "born", land in the garbage can.

Talcum Powder

Inaccurate Copy

As a mold release, you can use glycerine which, however, has a disadvantage in that it is very difficult to remove the glycerine for the mold. Another possibility is talcum powder. The third type of mold release is a mixture of 80 percent liquid soft soap and 20 percent acid free 4 percent oil. The mold release fluid is painted on in a very thin coat, since the plaster cannot penetrate into all of the cavities of the surface of the Wankelin model. An inaccurate copy will be produced when you use too much mold release; the mold release will lie between the plaster and the model.

Preparation of the Plaster

Plaster and water and mixed in proportion of nine parts water to eleven or twelve parts plaster. In a bucket where the correct amount of water is placed, you start pouring the sifted plaster with increasing speed into the bucket until it does not sink anymore, but remains in a small heap on top of the water. Next, by reaching to the bottom of the bucket, you can mix the plaster and water, crushing lumps with your fingers. The consistency of the plaster paste should resemble that of unbeaten cream. Let the bucket hit the work board several times so that the captured air bubbles will rise to the surface and escape. On no account during the hardening of the plaster paste is water allowed to be added, because otherwise through the chemical absorption of water, it will disrupt the hardening and the proper hardening is then disturbed.

Plaster Paste

Hardening

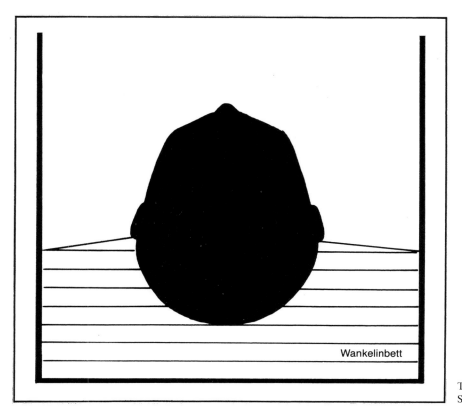

Wankelinbett

The embedding of the head with Wankelin. Slight sloping surface.

Divided Mold — Flange Neck Head

In order not to go into each mold separately, since the work procedures repeat themselves, I have confined myself to describing several basic procedures based on the example of the flange neck head.

Neck Ring

Lay the flange neck head onto the laminated plywood board. With a piece of Wankelin, produce a bed for the head so that the head is embedded into the Wankelin. The ring of the neck and the opening of the pouring hole should lie vertically, since the neck opening will be later sealed with the plexiglass pane, ensuring that no plaster can run into this opening. Plaster is like water! It will always search for an opening!

Undercuts

Close the nostrils and other strong cavities, such as the corners of the mouth or ears, with Wankelin (undercuts).

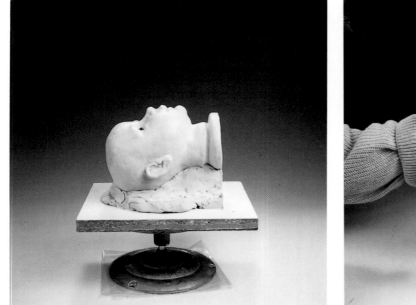

Embed the head with modeling clay. Make sure that the neck opening is vertical.

Close the nostrils with modelling clay.

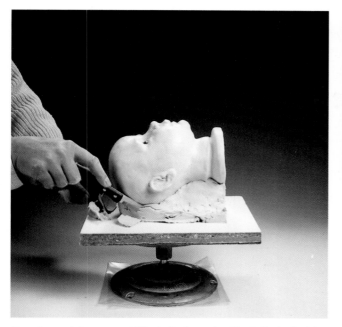

Cut all remaining rests of Wankelin from the Wankelin bed with a sharp knife.

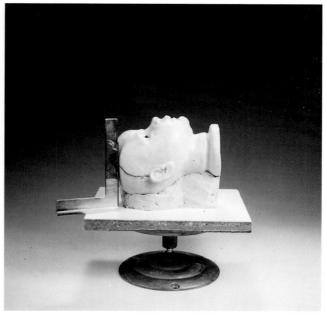

Once more draw the line with a pencil so that it is clearly visible.

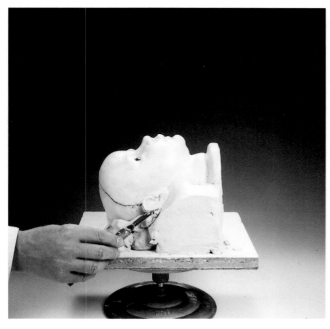

The lower part of the head is embedded as far as the dividing line with Wankelin. The Wankelin bed is built up so that the head lies horizontally.

The Wankelin should surround the head with a 2in (5cm) overlapping border. Smooth out the Wankelin very carefully with talcum powder so that later both halves of the mold lie smoothly together.

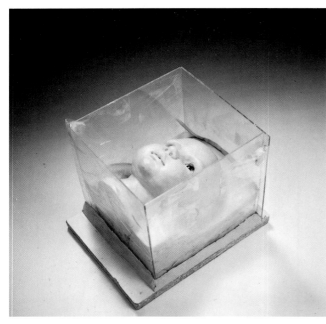

Four plexiglass panes are placed around the embedded head.

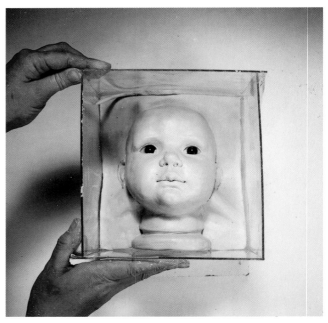

The glass panes should be at right angles to each other.

The glass panes are then wrapped tightly around with tape.

To make it water tight, seal all cracks and openings with modelling clay so that the plaster cannot flow out. Mark a point on the glass which is 1¹⁄₈ to 1⁵⁄₈in (3 to 4cm) higher than the highest point of the model head.

With the already prepared plaster paste and a brush, dab the eyes. Pour in the plaster paste, beginning at the lowest point and filling it up to the highest previously marked point.

Pour the plaster paste steadily and without setting it down.

With a long handled brush, carefully start brushing in the mold and on the head so that all air bubbles can rise.

After approximately one hour, the plaster will have hardened and you can now remove the plexiglass panes. Turn the plaster mold on its back and free the head from the Wankelin.

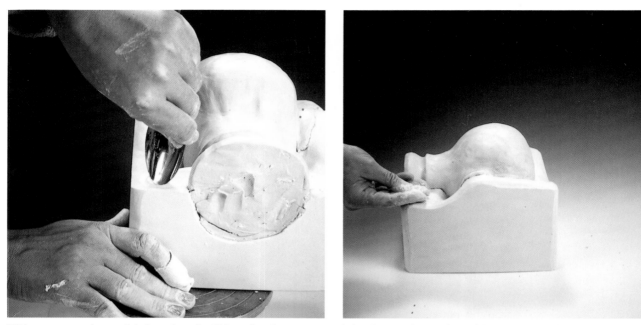

With a spoon, make small indentations (lock) into the plaster.

Paint the complete surface with a thin layer of mold release.

The plexiglass frames are again placed around the head as described before and bound tightly with tape.

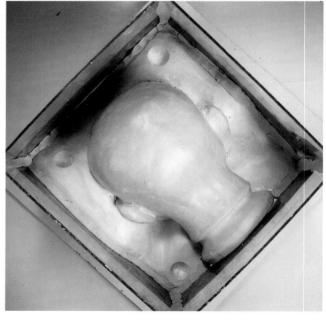

Cracks are sealed and the plaster paste is poured in. After one hour, the glass can be removed.

Careful! Danger of injuries! Break off the sharp corners of the mold with a metal spatula.

The mold lies flat on the board in front of you with the face looking up. To remove the top part of the mold, you have to take a hammer and rubber wedge and pry open the four corners.

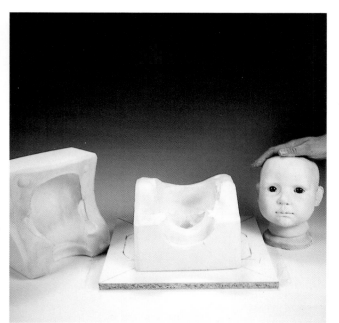

Before you can use the mold for the first time, it must dry for about eight days.

Remove the model head.

Rough Cast Mold — Breast Plate Head

The rough cast mold which I would like to demonstrate to you with the aid of the model head with the molded-on breast plate is made in three parts. Rough cast molds have the disadvantage that they cannot be used often. However, they happen to be the easiest type to make and, therefore, are especially suitable for producing originals (single piece, doll only made once). The ears of this model are far more deeply modelled out. That is why the mold is made in three parts. You do not close the ears with Wankelin, but instead, let the plaster run into the undercuts. With a three-piece mold you can take the mold parts in which the ears are made away from the sides, saving you from making a more complicated four-piece mold which normally is necessary with well-modelled ears.

Lay the head down as already described onto the work board and establish and mark the dividing line on both mold parts using an angle iron before embedding it in Wankelin. ▶

The second dividing line runs from the rear of the head in a vertical line down the spine. ▶▶

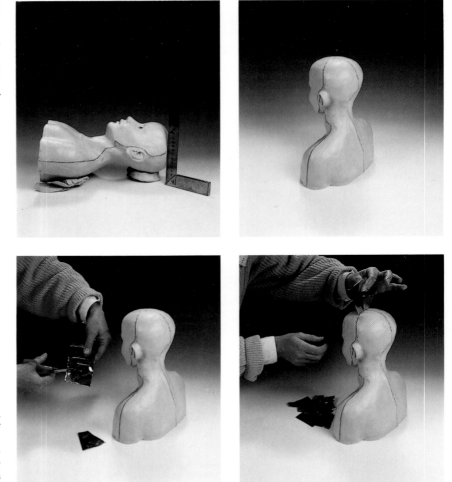

Prepare wedges made out of a copper sheet. ▶

These wedges are then pressed into the dividing line of the Wankelin model approximately ¹/₈in (3mm) deep, so that a "halo" is produced. ▶▶

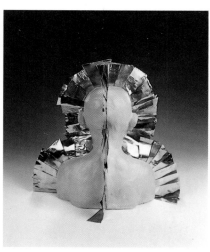

These metal wedges have to be so closely placed that the individual wedges overlap, ensuring a perfect separation of the mold parts.

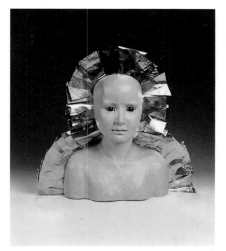

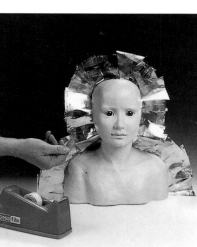

For safety reasons, tape the individual metal wedges together.

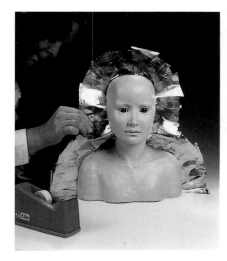

The head is now placed into a low carton lined with plastic wrap.

With this type of mold, it is advisable to work with several helpers.

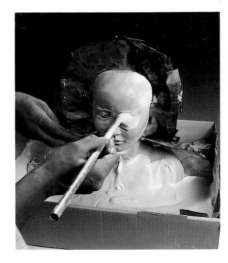 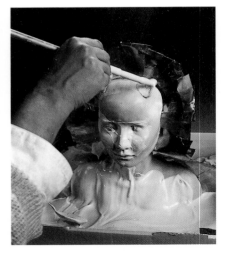

The prepared plaster is appropriately thrown on with the hand, spoon or spatula.

Before you begin throwing on the plaster, dab the eyes, nose and lips, as previously described, no air bubbles can be trapped below the undercuts.

Throw on small amounts of plaster from top to bottom on your Wankelin model. You can reach the smallest cavity of your model by blowing the plaster and thus obtain an exact copy in the plaster.

After you have applied the first layer, you can use your hands to aid the process.

Keep on placing the plaster on until the wedges are covered. With a metal spatula, smooth out the wet plaster.

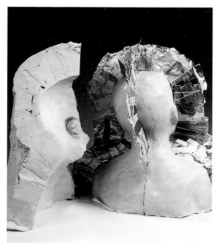

After approximately one hour, the plaster should have hardened. On several of the higher seams, the metal wedges are removed using pliers. In these gaps begin pouring water, little by little, until the mold parts come easily apart.

Mold Making Socket Head

Four-Part Mold

Blank

I will now demonstrate with the aid of a socket head how a four-part mold is produced. As already described, the ears of the model head are thoroughly modelled out for the four-part mold, and when making the mold a wedge piece (wedge piece = additional mold part, suitable for mold making models with undercuts) is produced for each ear. Then the ears of the blank only have to be cleaned and polished.

Construct a bed of Wankelin for the head so that it has a good support. With the angle iron, circle the head and establish the dividing line, which is then clearly marked. Note that with this dividing line, the ears are separately marked with a pencil. The highest point is not established with the angle iron or pencil on the ear, but they are encircled. Therefore, the dividing line runs once over the ear and once below.

The Wankelin lower bed is now built up to the dividing line and should surround the head with an overlapping frame about ³/₄ to 1¹/₄in (2 to 3cm) deep.

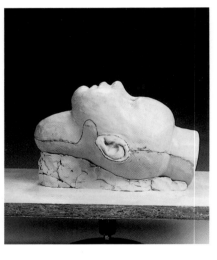

The lamenated plywood boards do not surround the Wankelin like with the flange neck head. (The ears are completely covered with Wankelin). The Wankelin bed, which ends at the upper seam, must be completely smooth on the surface.

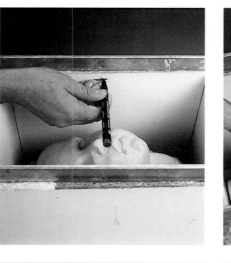

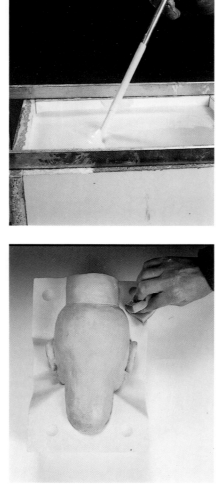

Here we use for the construction a completely different technique. Four lamenated plywood boards are placed at right angles around the embedded head. However, these boards do not touch with the Wankelin bed; on the contrary, the distance to the doll head depends upon the size of the mold which can be between 1⁵/₈in (4cm) and 3⁷/₈in (10cm). The pouring hole for the porcelain is created by the Wankelin structure on top of the head. This structure must be sealed off by the board so that a hole appears in the plaster mold through which the porcelain material can be poured. The boards are fastened together with screw clamps. The cracks are filled up with Wankelin. With a pencil, mark the filling level. This is a point which lies approximately 1¹/₈in (3cm) above the highest point of the head. Now pour this plaster up to this point and stir it with a long-handled paintbrush so that the air bubbles are removed. After one hour, the plaster is cold and has hardened. Now you can remove the boards. Turn the plaster square onto its back and remove the Wankelin bed. Remove the overlapping plaster with a hammer and chisel. With the knife, cut out the rest of the remaining plaster right up to the clearly marked dividing line. Try to smooth the upper surface of the mold as cleanly as possible with a knife. With sandpaper and a scouring sponge, you can get a far better result. After this process, locks are made into the plaster with a spoon.

The ear, which was uncovered from the Wankelin, is once again embedded up to the dividing line with Wankelin.

Brush the back of the head as well as the plaster with a thin coat of mold release. The lamenated plywood boards are replaced and fastened and the cracks are again fillled up. The plaster paste is poured in and the air bubbles are removed by stirring.

 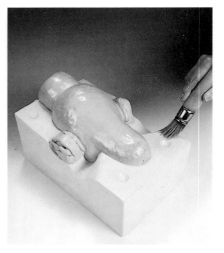

After the second half of the plaster has hardened, the boards are removed. The Wankelin remaining over the ear is also removed, without damaging the mold or ear. It is necessary that you turn both mold halves around. Both mold halves are held together with two boards and screw clamps so that during this process they do not fall apart. The created cavities are brushed with mold release and are then filled with plaster. The ear wedges are hardened after one hour. With a metal spatula, break open the edges of the mold.

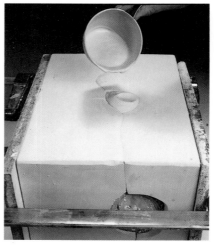 

Remove the ear wedges laterally.

For preserving, close the mold with mold bands.

 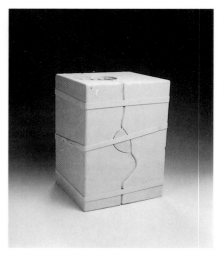

The Breast Plate Procedure

Dividing Line

Undercut

Neck Opening

Embed the breast plate as such so that the breast is turned upwards. With an angle iron, make your dividing line and then draw the line so that it is clearly seen. Up to this you build your Wankelin bed. This Wankelin bed should surround the breast with a depth of ⁵⁄₈ to ³⁄₄in (1.5 to 2 cm). the curved indentation, in which the neck is later placed, is now closed with a curved Wankelin stopper so that no undercuts are created. Surround the embedded Wankelin breast with lamenated plywood boards and fasten them with screw clamps. Pour in the prepared plaster. Stir to remove any air bubbles. After one hour, remove the boards, the Wankelin bed and stopper. Smooth out the upper surface of the mold with a knife or sandpaper. Now the first half of the mold is finished. Using the spoon, make locks into the plaster. The next step is to cast the wedge for the opening. The neck opening was that part which was closed with the Wankelin stopper before the first part of the mold was made. Place two thin Wankelin wedges at the neck opening; both run outwards to the board and are a little higher than the neck opening. You should make sure that no plaster can leak out at the wedges. Before you pour the plaster into the neck and between the wedges, you must paint the parts with mold remover. Otherwise, you cannot remove the wedge from the mold half. After the plaster wedge is casted, remove the wedge from the mold half. After the plaster wedge is casted, wait for about one hour until the plaster has hardened. Remove the boarded frame. Then remove the wedge and process it as follows: trace a dividing line and from this line, with a sharp knife, cut away downwards and to the inside of the lower half and both side parts approximately ³⁄₈ to ³⁄₄in (1 to 2 cm). Brush the wedge and the first mold half with mold remover. Once again it is surrounded with boards and the second half of the mold is casted with plaster. After removing the boards, separate both mold halves as described and take out the plaster wedge. The result is a three-part mold, namely the two mold halves and the plaster wedge. When casting with this mold, all three pieces are held together with mold bands. When separating after 1¹⁄₂ to 2 hours, first lift one mold half off, then remove the wedge. After this, the blank can be removed from the second half of the mold.

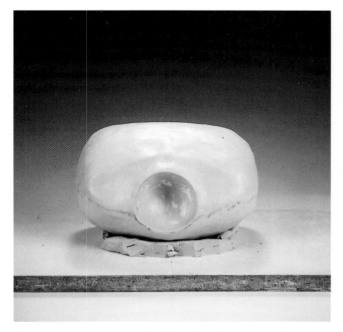

Embed the breast plate with Wankelin. The breast plate faces upwards.

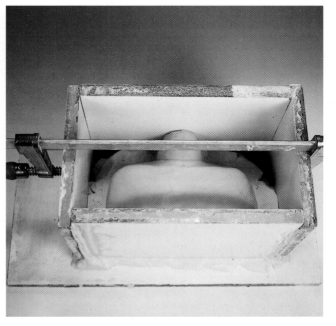

Seal the neck opening with a Wankelin stopper. The model is surrounded with laminated plywood boards.

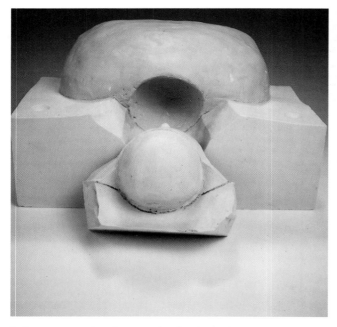

Before you cast the plaster wedge for the neck opening, brush the other mold parts with mold remover.

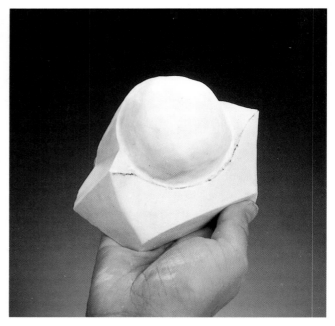

Going out from the drawn line, cut away the lower half and both side parts approximately ³/₈ to ³/₄in (1 to 2cm) with a sharp knife.

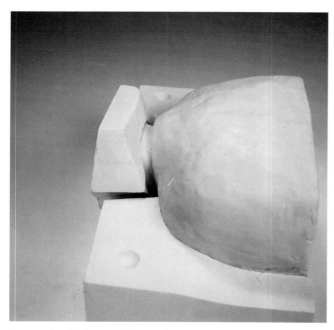

To cast the third part of the mold, replace the plaster wedge.

This is how the three parts of the mold look.

Dream Dancer ▶

Mold Making Of The Arms And Legs

There is no difference in how the arms and legs should be embedded. For this reason, a one-time description is enough. Make sure when making the molds of the limbs that the right leg and right arm are always made with their opposite counterpart in the same mold. Thus, no mistakes can be made. Both the arms and legs are embedded in a Wankelin bed. It is important that no undercuts are created. With an angle iron, established the dividing line. The modelled bed should be very smooth and should reach each spot of the dividing line. It is left up to you if you want to use laminated plywood boards fastened with screw clamps of plexiglass panes wrapped around with tape. Place the frame of your choice around the embedded limbs and fasten them. On the wall of your frame mark a point approximately 2in (5cm) above the highest point of the embedded limbs. It is advisable to brush the whole bed of the modelling clay and the limbs with a thin layer of mold removeer so that later they are easier to remove from the mold. It is not a must, but can be helpful. Now pour in the plaster up to the filling mark. The plaster was prepared as described before. Remove the air bubbles with a long handled paintbrush. After cooling and hardening of the plaster, you now can remove either the glass or the boards. Next, turn the block around until the Wankelin bed faces upwards; remove the Wankelin bed. Make four locks with a spoon in the mold, at each corner. The limbs plus the mold half are now painted with a thin layer of mold remover. This painting is never to be forgotten. If it is, then the hardened plaster will bind with fresh plaster and will lock your limbs in. The surrounding frame is once more placed around the block. Pour the plaster in up to the filling mark. After cooling and hardening, remove the frame and open the mold using a hammer and a rubber wedge. Lift the upper mold half vertically into the air. To avoid hurting oneself, it is advisable to break off the sharp corners of the mold.

Preparation of the hand mold. The modelled hand is now embedded in the modelling clay. Observe the dividing line.

The hands in the first mold half.

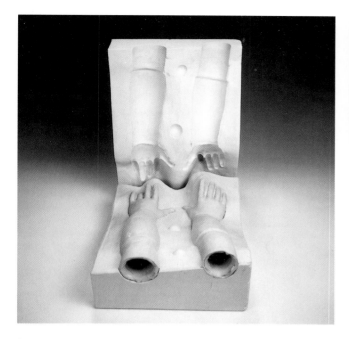

Opened mold of the hands. Mold is clearly seen.

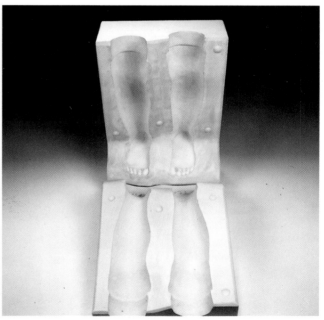

With help of an angle iron, the dividing line is established.

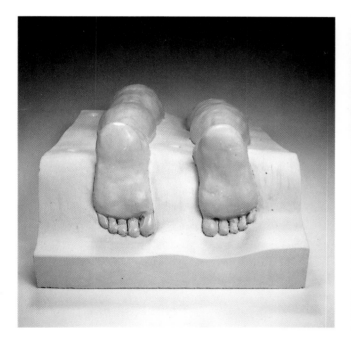

Opened leg mold with inlaid model legs.

Cast both legs in one mold. No confusion is possible.

*Chapter 4*_____

Porcelain

Before you even begin with the work, I would like to warn you about the careless relationship with porcelain material.

Kaolin

Porcelain contains a substance called kaolin which should not be inhaled. The porcelain dust created from rubbing and grinding will settle in the bronchials and you can get pneumoconiosis! Always work with a dust mask and buy a suction fan when a lot of porcelain is to be ground.

Dust Mask

You can ban this danger in the summertime by working outside. To prevent the dust from settling into the pores and on the skin of the face, rub a fatty cream on yourself before work begins. Once finished, clean your face, arms and hands well so that no skin impurities or allergies are created.

The best way of protecting oneself is clean work when making the molds.

The Casting Procedure

Mold Bands

After you have placed the mold flat down in front of you and have removed the mold bands, with your thumbs test the corners to see whether both parts will separate without any trouble.

If this is the case, place both hands at the sides of the upper mold half and carefully lift straight upwards. Do not use any force. Otherwise you may damage the mold.

If the mold does not separate without problems, then take a fine brush or sponge, moisten it with water and rub into the cracks of the mold. After a few minutes you can then remove the upper part of the mold. Again, never use force or you may damage the mold.

After separating, you must thoroughly check whether the inside of the mold is free of plaster particles, dust or other small things which may later be seen on the porcelain.

Now brush the inside of the mold with a soft clean brush. Do not touch the mold with your fingers. You may accidently make scratches with your fingernails.

List of materials: Mold, porcelain material, mold bands, soft thick brush, scalpel, container or plastic bowl with spout, strainer, spoon for stirring.

The mold should not be dry. You have the option of using an atomizer and spraying a little amount of water into the mold. Make sure that there is not too much water in the mold!

On the table in front of you you have the lower part of the mold. Both molds are clean. Place the other part carefully back on with the sides being flush.

Atomizer

The Porcelain Material

You need a stirring spoon for the preparation of the porcelain material so that it can be well mixed, since a part of this liquid will settle at the bottom. Pour the porcelain through a strainer into a container and after stirring once again, let it stand for a while until all the air bubbles have risen. This careful preparation is very necessary, if you do not want to have any unevenness on your finished head.

Stirring

Unevenness

The noticeable crack between the mold is approximately $1/16$ to $1/8$ in (2 to 3mm) deep. This is for catching hold of when taking apart the mold. The inside of the mold closes seamless.

Let the material stand long enough until no more air bubbles (pin-sized, black points) are seen on the surface.

Close the mold again using the mold bands. The side which has the face is marked with the word "top", because the porcelain parts in a hard leather condition will later be worked on in the mold. If the face is pointing downwards, then one cannot start work in the mold.

Casting

Casting Hole

Place the mold with the casting hole facing upwards on your work board. The prepared porcelain material is once more stirred so that still existing air bubbles are removed.

Now lift your container slowly up and pour the material into the hole.

Porcelain material is poured back.

You must make sure when pouring that you pour steadily and without setting the mold down. Every time you set it down, delay rings are made which remain visible on the fired head even when cleaned.

Delaying Rings

Let the mold stand for about a minute and you will notice that the material is settling down. Pour some more porcelain and wait again several minutes. After a short time, you will see on the walls of the opening that a "skin" has formed.

The plaster mold is removing fluids from the porcelain material; the material is hardening. What thickness the head should have depends upon you, before the remaining liquid is poured back. A larger head must have a thicker wall than a smaller one. How fast the porcelain material hardens cannot be foreseen since there are many factors like the condition of the mold (dry or moist), room temperature and humidity which influence this process.

Thickness

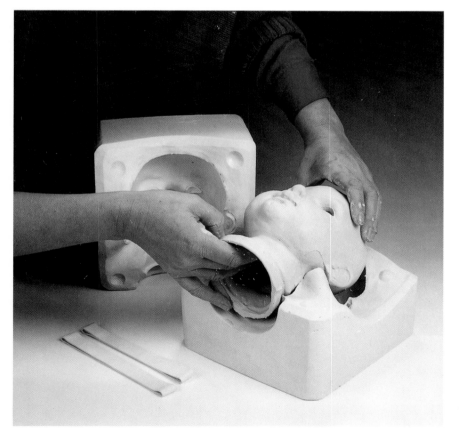

Careful removal of the head from the mold (demolding) in a hard leather condition.

When the wanted thickness is reached, pour the remaining liquid porcelain material back into the container. So as not to miss the moment for pouring back, either observe the mold constantly or if you happen to go away, set an alarm clock.

Pour your material out of the mold in the same way you poured it in. Do not let the material come "blubbering" out. If this happens, a vacuum could develop, meaning that the head may collapse, making the whole cast unusable.

After pouring the liquid back, turn the mold so that the hole is pointing downward towards the strainer, enabling the rest to be collected. The remaining porcelain material is poured back into the closed container and can be used again.

The Demolding

Casted porcelain parts should remain in the mold for at least one hour. If you remove the upper mold half to early, it is possible that the parts will still be wet and they can easily tear. Casted porcelain parts which dry in the mold shrink. This makes it easier when you separate the mold halves from each other. You should not let the cast stand for more than one day because the casted parts may dry out too much and the danger arises that small pieces may break off when demolding. When you remove the porcelain from the mold, it has a grayish color and it has a condition of "hard leather." After five to eight days, the head dries out so much that it becomes white. Porcelain parts which have not been fired are called "blanks."

Lay the mold with the marked upper side in front of you. Remove the mold bands and lift the upper mold slowly upwards so that the head does not get damaged.

The cast is still lying in the lower mold. You leave it there until you have removed the edges of the molding hole with a scalpel from either head or neck.

Should your doll receive glass eyes, it is advisable that the eyes be cut out while it is still in a "hard leather" condition, since with a dried "blank," it is very easy to break out pieces. To finally remove the cast from the mold, clean your hands so that the head does not get dirty. Lift up the mold in which the cast is still lying, tilt the mold and let the head, arms and legs fall carefully into your hands. Do not pry the parts from the mold using force. It may still be too wet. If so, it is advisable to let it dry for another half hour instead of forcing it. Doing so, you may crush the head or limbs.

Once you have removed the blank from the mold, you can now remove the "seams" with a scalpel. These "seams" are created where the two mold halves came together and must be carefully removed when cleaned because, when fired, they may "rise" and become visible.

Besides the seams, also the edges of the pouring hole (top of head , extended leg) have to be removed. After the demolding of the flange neck head, for example, you should not forget to remove the back plate of the head with a scalpel so that when completing the doll, the eyes can be easily inserted into the head.

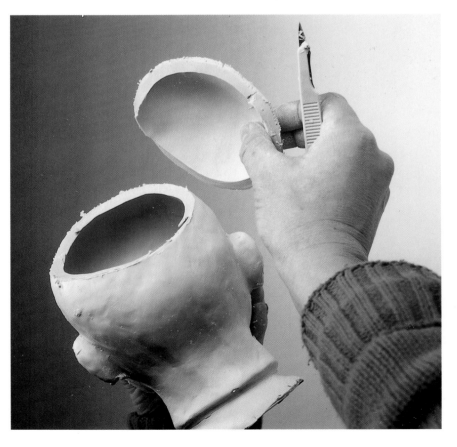

Cleaning

After two to three days, the dried "blank" can be cleaned. You must handle it with care since it is breakable like a raw egg. For cleaning you need: dust mask!, scalpel, hard brush, soft brush, eye socket tools, organza silk or nylon stocking and a scouring sponge.

You first cut the seams away with a scalpel. The edges of the eyes must also be cut out clean and evenly with a scalpel. The precision work on the eyes is first done with a hard brush, which you use for smoothing the edges of the eye opening.

The next thing you need is the eye socket tool, which is wrapped in organza silk or a nylon stocking and serves to smooth out very thinly the inner edges of the eye sockets of the head, using light pressure and a twisting motion.

The rest of the unevenness is removed by gently rubbing on the blank with the silk organza cloth, which is wrapped around the finger. The ears are modelled again with a hard brush or scalpel and then rubbed smoothly.

With the legs and arms, scratch out the nails with the scalpel. The most important part are the holes, which are made using the scalpel, bored into the porcelain parts and used for sewing onto the body. These are the arms, legs and breast plate. Do not forget the holes in the neck curve of the socket head and breast plate so that when the doll is completed, both parts can be joined. Scratch your name and the date in the nape of the neck of the doll. Every artist should sign his name on his work! Finally, clean the head from the porcelain dust with a soft brush because when firing, each speck of dust will be fired along and will remain forever on the finished doll as a sign of ugliness.

◀ With the help of a scalpel, open the back of the head so that after the head has been fired and painted, the glass eyes can be mounted.

Material for cleaning the porcelain: dust mask, scouring sponge, organza silk, hard brush, scalpel and eye socket tool.

Holes in the Casted Porcelain Head

When you cast your mold several times and always the same holes appear on the porcelain head, it is a sign that in the mold there are several plaster lumps enclosed, whose insides are still powdery. This means that within these lumps the plaster has not yet set with water. When casting, the plaster mold absorbs the moisture from the porcelain. Those unset plaster lumps are also penetrated by moisture. The locked-in air is forced to escape since it is pushed out by the water; it, therefore, finds its way into the porcelain and causes holes to occur.

So that the plaster lumps can be set, lay the mold into the water for a short time. Remove it when no air rises. Then let it dry for several days.

Repairing Faulty Spots on the Casted Porcelain Head

It is possible even with careful work, that the already casted porcelain parts show holes. These come about when preparing the porcelain material, since not all of the air bubbles have escaped.

The holes, which have been created, can be repaired by dipping a fine brush into the porcelain material and filling up these holes. From cavities there are now ridges, which can be removed by cleaning and smoothing.

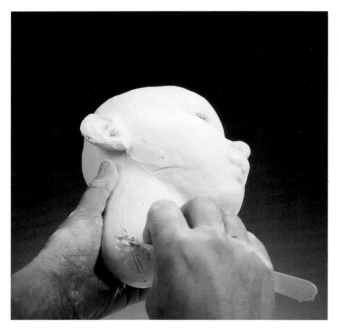

Remove casting seams with a scalpel.

Clean the ears.

The eyes are cut out with a scalpel.

Pull a piece of nylon stocking over the eye socket tool so that the eyes can be cleaned from the inside. The eye socket tool can also be used as a control to see if the glass eye will fit since the eye and the tool have an alike curve.

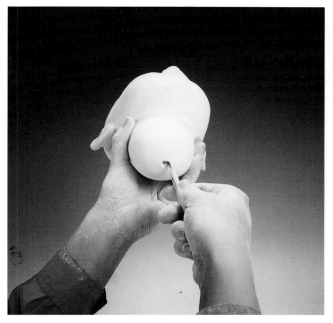

Bore a hole using the scalpel so that the head can be connected to the breast plate.

Work very carefully so that no porcelain pieces break off.

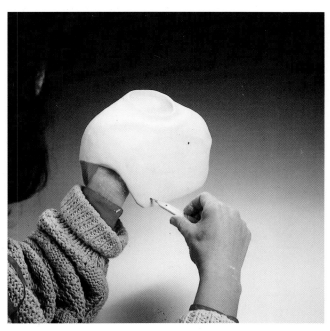

The four holes of the breast plate are bored with a scalpel. These are used later for connecting the breast plate to the body.

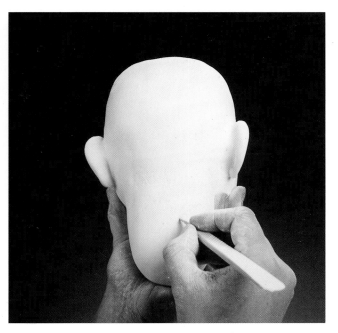

Scratch in the name of the artist, doll's name, the number of the doll (when in series) and year.

*Chapter 5*_____

Firing

Kiln

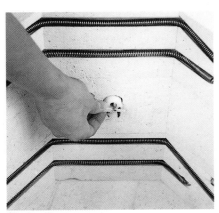

Placing the temperature cone.

For the firing procedure, press the button of the drop in.

For firing the porcelain you need a kiln, whose temperature can reach up to 1260°C. For firing skin colored and black colored porcelain, a temperature of 1220°C is enough but if you want to work with white porcelain as well, then you must make sure that you have a firing temperature that lies at 1260°C.

Firing can also be done at hobby shops but it is recommended that you purchase such a kiln as a one-time investment, especially if you work often with porcelain.

A lot of kilns are offered in various price ranges. For your own hobby a kiln with a volume of 28 liters is sufficient. Kilns of this size can, without any difficulty, be set up in your own home since they feed off the normal electrical circuit.

A kiln is either electronically steered or through a control unit with temperature cones. I myself use the smaller kiln (28 liters), which is fitted out with a half automatic and works on the principle of temperature cones. With the aid of this system with which I have had the most experience, I will explain how to operate this kiln.

Temperature cones are small cones which are placed by hand into the kiln and control the temperature. After reaching the required temperature, the kiln automatically shuts off. This type of function is for this reason called a "half-automatic."

Temperature cones have a firing range between 600° and 1300°C and can be bought for each temperature. This means that in addition to porcelain, you can also fire enamel, clay, ceramic, and so forth.

The exact operating instructions are included with the kiln when you buy it; therefore I will only explain the basic principles of firing.

Placing of the Temperature Cone and Controls

The cone is placed by hand onto the cone support in the inside of the kiln. The firing rod lies on top of the cone.

1. The drop on the outside of the kiln's control unit is folded upwards and the firing rod is locked into place.

2. Due to this, the firing rod on the inside of the kiln moves upwards and the cone can be set into place.

3. Important: Since the cone is the release element which shuts off the kiln, it is important that it is correctly placed for a proper firing. The kiln must stand on a flat surface.

4. If the cone is unintentionally moved or comes into contact with the porcelain wall, it is possible that the firing will be too high and too long, which could ruin your kiln!

So that the kiln will shut off at the right time, it is very important to adjust it correctly. That is why two test cones 020 are delivered with the kiln. Lay one of these into the kiln as described and turn it on to "full." After depressing the white plastic button into the drop-release, a red control lamp lights up. The kiln is now functioning. After 30 to 35 minutes, the kiln turns off automatically. Look at the cone. The cone must be burnt through at a 90° angle. Normally the kiln is adjusted when it leaves the factory; however, through transportation and so forth, it may have altered slightly. If the cone is not burnt through at a right angle, you can make an adjustment rather easily. Loosen the correction screw on the ouside of the drop-release and shift the metal plate minimally. Before shifting it, mark its original position so that if the metal plate falls out or if it is moved too far, you know at least where the starting point is. Adjust the screw and make another test to see whether the cone is burnt through at a right angle.

If the cone is bent too little, adjust the metal plate upwards. If it is bent too strongly, adjust the metal plate downwards. This has to be done until the right adjustment (right angle) is found.

After the firing procedure, the drop-release falls down.

The Firing of Bisque

Before you load the kiln, make sure that all the porcelain parts to be fired are well dried out. Raw porcelain should dry for about five days; larger pieces under some circumstances should dry somewhat longer.

Use the kiln sand, which you can buy, to protect the heads from deformation. Spread about 3/8in (1cm) of sand on the bottom or on the plates and place the heads on top of the sand.

Keep a distance of about 1 1/8in (3cm) from the measuring rod and 3/4in (2cm) from the kiln wall. There should also be a small gap between the parts to be fired.

After the firing, do not immediately open the kiln! Wait for at least two hours; then open the top approximately 7/16in (1cm) and place a support in the opening. After another three to four hours, you can open it completely. It would even be better to let the oven cool off overnight.

This procedure is for the full firing. With colored firing, the time can be shortened to two hours before opening.

*Chapter 6*_____

Painting

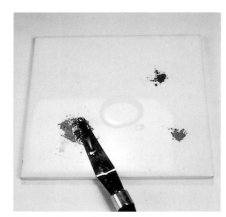

Mixing of the colors.

There are a lot of doll artists who found the entrance to this hobby whilst they began to produce reproductions of antique dolls.

When making reproductions, it is very important that the painting is identical to that of the original doll. This requires an exact knowledge of using colors and mixed oils and presumes an exact working method.

With the painting of your own artist doll, you do not have to follow a pattern. It remains up to you how you want to do it and with what colors and oils you want to paint your doll. For a long time now I have not followed any specific rules. This is only possible through much experimentation to find your own complete individual method of painting.

Material for painting: porcelain colors, oil mix, paint brushes in various thicknesses (cat's tongue, stippler, and so forth), palette knife (narrow spatula for mixing), glazed tile or glass plate and foam rubber wrapped in silk.

I will now introduce to you a small insight into the wide spectrum of oils, colors and their uses. Every doll does not only need an appropriate wig, appropriate eyes and clothes but also the right skin color.

I do not want to limit your artistic freedom by giving you painting instructions. That is why you should take my recommendations to this topic as being only a reference.

Try to keep to human examples and biological realities. Try to avoid, for example, painting a blonde child with black eyelashes and eyebrows. It is usual with red-haired dolls to paint a light complexion, sometimes also with freckles.

To give further examples is useless. You should try in any case to strive for an outer harmony. Imagine you are sitting at a concert listening to a quiet melody and at the most unsuitable moment, a trumpet blows. This is how it seems to a doll lover when a certain type of doll head is painted with the wrong colors.

Different color shades.

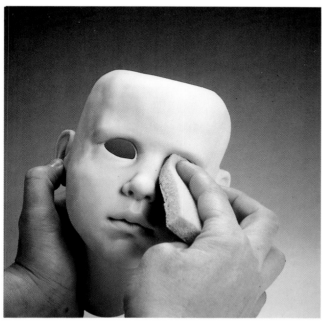

The porcelain must be well smoothed with a grit scrubber.

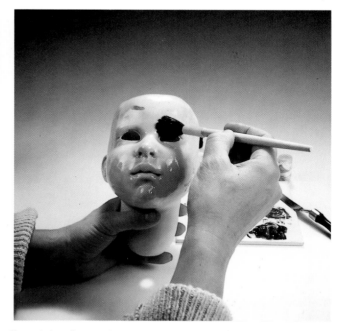

Spread the oil over the complete face.

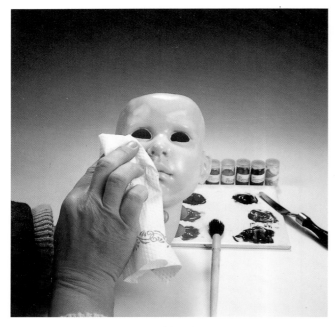

Too much oil can be removed with a tissue.

After the first color firing at 720°C, you can again darken the shade of the head.

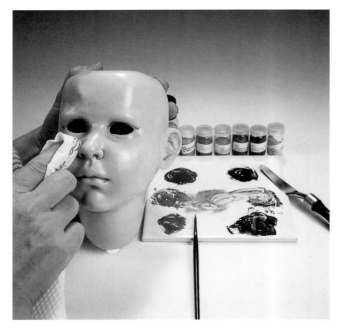

Distribute the color evenly over the face.

Through applying various shades, you obtain a very life-like color of the face.

Color stresses the depth and lines of the modelling.

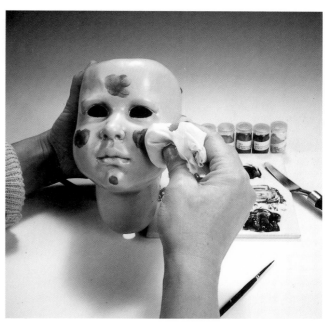

Choice of cheek red, purple and pompadour-red, depending upon type.

The cheek red is evenly distributed with a silk swab.

Too much red color is again removed.

The eyebrows are painted stroke-by-stroke with a fine long-haired brush. I mix the colors of the eyebrows, lashes and mouth with copaiva oil.

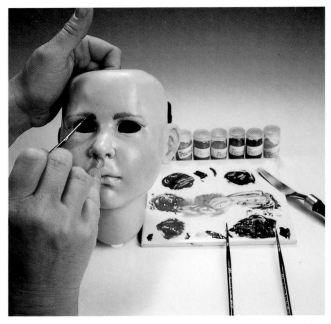

The color of the eyebrows should be appropriate with the color of the doll's hair.

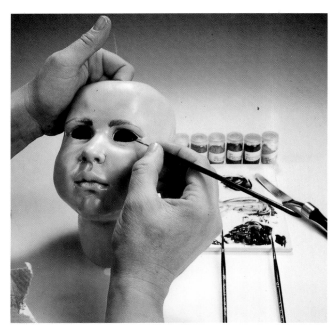

The lashes are painted with a natural curve.

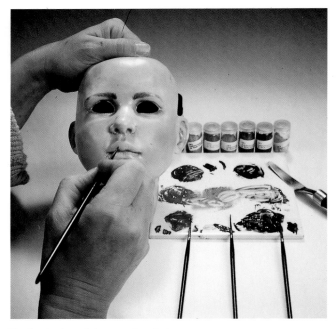

The beginning of the mouth painting.

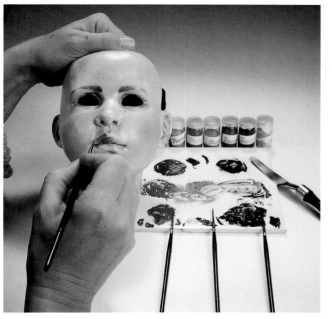

Apply a warm red color onto the lips. For this a cat's tongue brush is suitable.

Pay attention to the painting of the lips — keep to a clean border.

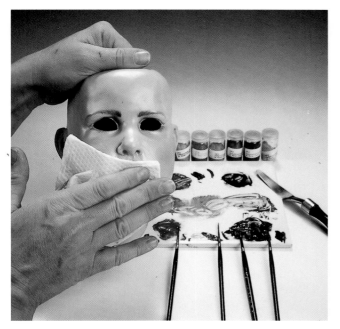

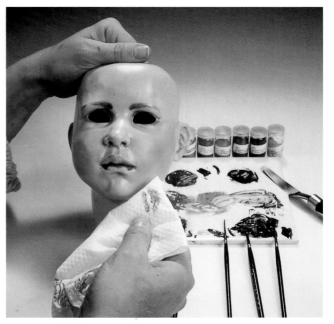

Remove unneccessary paint from the mouth with a tissue.

The lighter the shade, the more natural the doll appears.

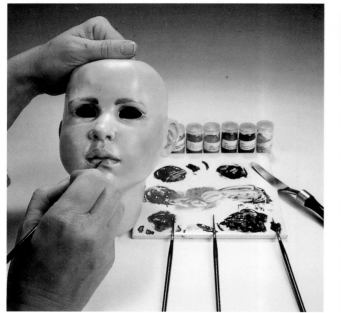

Puckered lips and cracks are deepened with little color and the very finest brush.

Finished painted head.

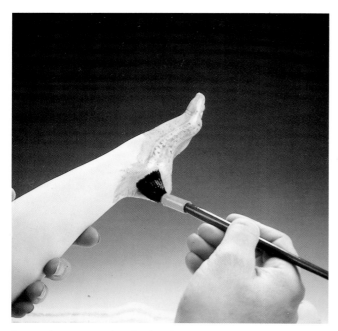

Legs and arms are painted using the same procedure.

Apply a very soft shade for the fingernails.

Doll child in original size. ▶

*Chapter 7*_____

Completion

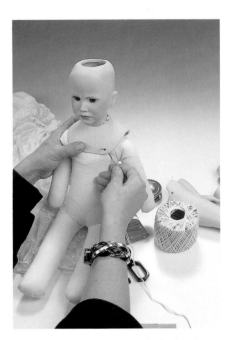

The breast plate is sewn onto the body using a rounded needle and strong thread. (Example: socket head *Georgina*).

Stuffing Material

For the completion, you need a body to which the limbs and the head are fastened. An all-porcelain doll requires high demands of the artistic and technical capabilities of a doll maker, which a beginner cannot justify. However, nobody has to forego with the body of his ideas. I myself do not have much time to provide my dolls with a porcelain body but have, just like most of the other doll makers who have gone over, accommodated most of my dolls with a cloth or leather body. You will find a pattern for a cloth body on page 101 (approximately ¹/₃ the size of the original pattern).

For the body you need muslin with a high firmness. Muslin can be bought in fabric shops. Sew the body according to the instructions and make very strong seams. Always remember that the body must be stuffed very tightly with stuffing material and, therefore, the seams have to hold up against this burden.

My experience has been that cotton-wool makes an excellent stuffing material. There is a cotton-wool which is tough and solid, the so-called magic cotton-wool, which is often used as packaging material.

This cotton-wool is predestined for stuffing doll bodies. If you use foam rubber as a stuffing, ugly humps form which disfigure the body. You may be able to find a stuffing which you prefer to cotton-wool such as sand or foam rubber. Regardless of which material you use, the body has to be packed solidly. The best thing you can use for this is a spoon without sharp edges with which you can stuff a cloth or leather body without mistakenly breaking through.

To the illustrations on page 95 from top to bottom:

A very strong glue is used for the flange neck ring. (Example: flange neck head *Baby Jenny*).

The sewn-together body is going to be connected to the head.

The head is tied into the body.

The Sewing on of the Various Types of Heads

The flange neck head is tied into the neck section. To be quite sure that when lifting the head, the doll does not fall out and break, it can be glued also as a safety measure. The head with the molded-on breast plate is sewn onto the body using the four holes in the breast plate.

The socket head is usually the most difficult one to attach. I have developed a method with which all these problems seem to be solved. I use two curtain rings made of metal approximately 1¹/₄ to 1⁵/₈in (3 to 4cm) in diameter, elastic and a small piece of soft leather. The

diameter of the curtain rings depends upon the size of the doll. The head covering (pate) and the wig are not allowed to be attached before the socket head and the breast plate have been connected.

The flange neck head is tied into the body after the body is completed. With the head with the molded-on breast plate, it does not matter whether you put on the covering and the wig or you sew on the breast plate first.

To Connect the Socket Head to the Breast Plate

Place the socket head, the correct fitting breast plate and tools in front of you. Tie a knot into an approximately 6⁷/₈in (20cm) long elastic with a curtain ring so that the ring is sitting in the middle of the elastic and the ends are dangling free. Place both ends of the elastic from above into the head and through the hole of the neck opening.

Into the neck curve of the breast plate glue a piece of leather so that later when you connect the head to the neck, there is no friction between these parts. Take both ends of the elastic and put them through the hole of the neck in the breast plate. One end of the elastic you put through the second ring and tie both ends after pulling the elastic tight. The head should have enough tension so it fits snuggly into the breast plate and only moves when required.

The porcelain limbs are pulled over the cloth of the body and are sewn to the holes provided. For sewing it on, it is easier to use an upholstery or curved needle. Using a strong, three-to-four ply cotton thread, you only need five to six stitches to fasten the porcelain limbs adequately.

A second possibility is to tie the limbs into the body. This method requires no holes in the blank, but only flange rings on the arms and legs, just like with the flange neck head. However, this limits the movements of the doll.

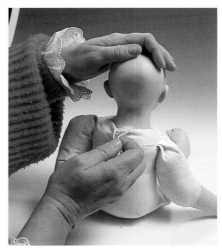

95

Flange Ring

If the flange ring lies on the upper arm and a certain arm movement is already modelled into it, the gracefulness of the doll is preserved. With a flange ring in the lower arm, which is glued and then tied into the cloth body, it looses its mobility.

If you put a sturdy wire through the cloth body, you can then fix the doll's positioning. That means, the doll does not hang in a stand, but can also take a dancer's position (see page 73).

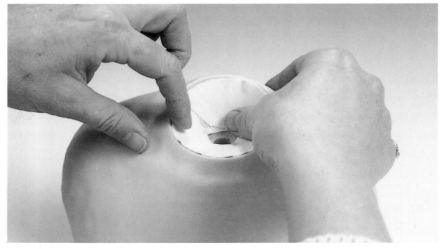

A piece of leather is glued into the breast plate.

Guide both elastic ends through the neck hole of the head.

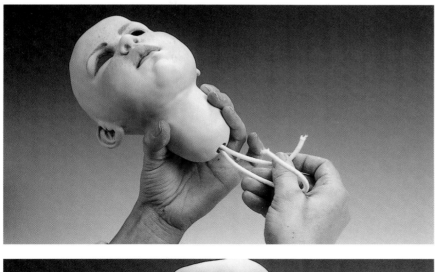

Pull both elastic ends tight...

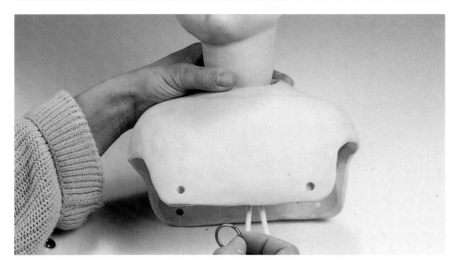

...and guide them through the hole of the breast plate.

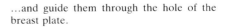

Place one end of the elastic through the second metal ring, pull tight and tie both ends together.

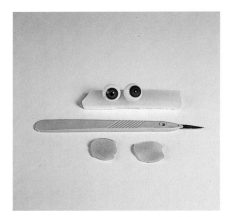

Material: eyes setting wax, scalpel, alabaster, bowl with spoon to mix the plaster, pate wig and glass eyes.

Inserting the Eyes - Attaching the Wig

The eyes are the soul of your doll. Do not try to be too economical when selecting the eyes. Your doll will thank you with a loving "glance." From the wax used for setting the eyes, tear off two small pieces. Knead these between your fingers until they are the thickness of a piece of paper. These wax discs are pressed into the eye sockets from the inside of the head. Cut the eye sockets free with a scalpel. A thin edge of wax remains around the eye on the inside of the head. Press the eyes into these edges. Hold the doll approximately 40in (100cm) in front of you and check whether the eyes of the doll are set straight. If necessary, correct them. Stir some plaster; lay the doll face down and set the eyes with the plaster from the inside of the head. You will need to use a small spoon so that no plaster runs into the head except that which is needed for setting the eyes. After one hour, the plaster will be set. Now you can use a moistened cotton swab to remove the remaining wax from the eyes. A papier-mache pate, available in different sizes, is attached to the head with tape. The wig is then attached to the pate using glue.

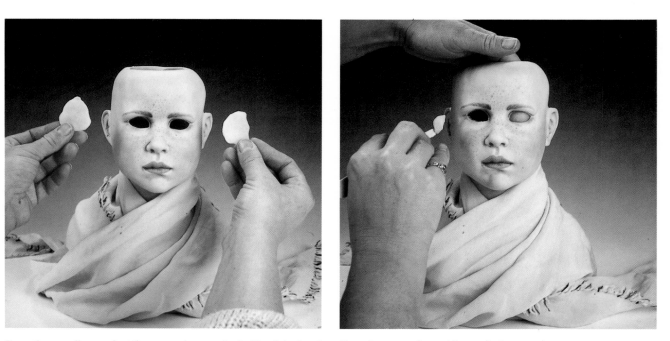

Press the wax discs against the eye sockets on the inside of the head.

Free the eye sockets with a scalpel.

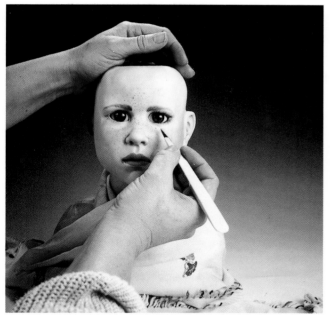

Insert the eyes. Remove remaining wax.

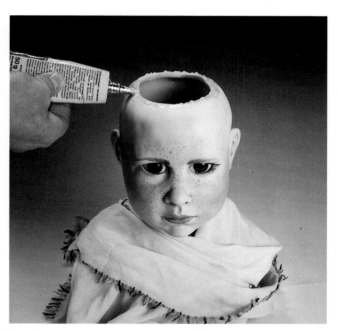

Put glue around the opening of the head.

Attach the pate.

Push back the hair of the wig so that no glue touches the hair; then place the wig onto the pate.

Lovely collectibles

Velvet, Silk, Lace

Clothing

You have taken continuous care that hands, feet and head position harmonize with each other. This harmony should also remain after the doll has been clothed. It is important that you listen to what your doll has to say. It can say, "Look here, I am a little coarse, come from the country and have a sturdy body." Or it can say, "Look at my fine limbs; I am a dancer." After what your doll has told you, you should then arrange the clothing and the accessories. You cannot place a nickel pair of glasses on the nose of a dancer and a cream-colored velvet suit is not appropriate for a coarse red-faced farmer's boy.

Velvet, silk and lace, whether old or new, can be combined with each other. There are a lot of old silk ribbons which sometime or another appear. Grab them; learn how to bargain and fight for the rare pieces which some other passionate doll maker wants to have. Only the best is good enough for your own self-made porcelain doll!

From old nightgowns and bed linen which you can find at flea markets, you can remove the lace and sew wonderful underwear or underskirts for your dolls. Maybe you have learned how to paint silk. This is also a possibility for designing your own wonderful clothing. You can also dye your own materials or if you prefer not to use chemicals, you can use tea or onion peel instead.

Play with cloths, colors and ribbons! Decorate the dresses of the dolls with feathers or flowers! Look for old doll handbags, shoes and hats! Let your creativity fly freely!

There are so many books which show the fashion of the past century. Turn over the pages of these books! You may have a wig which comes from the rococo period. Sew a matching dress in this style for your doll. Really, there is no lack of fantasy when you let yourself be encouraged from these books and photographs, but do not forget that the present day also offers a lot of ideas.

Hand-painted silk dress made from the pattern on pages 102-103.

Pattern for a Doll Body

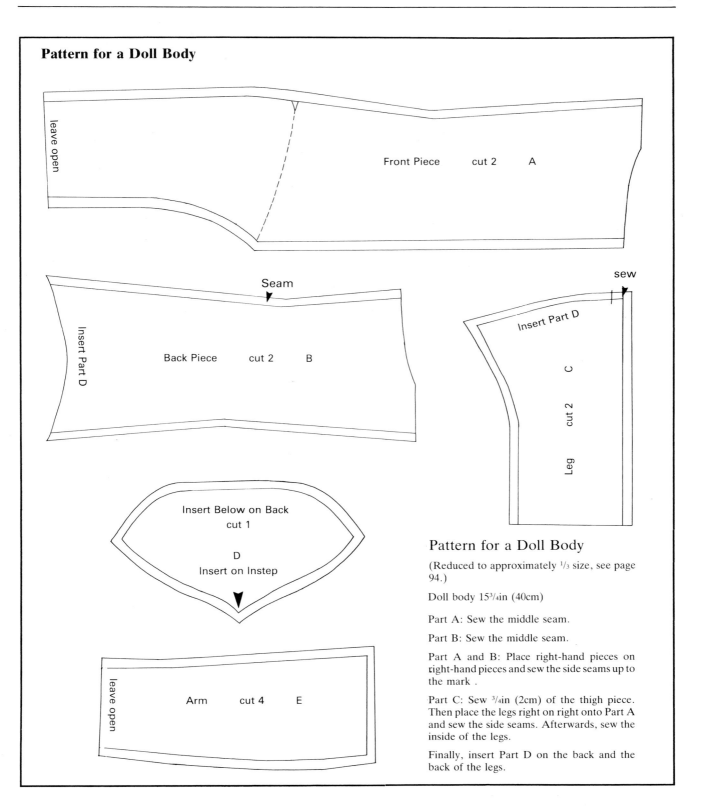

leave open

Front Piece   cut 2   A

Seam

Insert Part D

Back Piece   cut 2   B

sew

Insert Part D

Leg   cut 2   C

Insert Below on Back
cut 1

D

Insert on Instep

leave open

Arm   cut 4   E

Pattern for a Doll Body

(Reduced to approximately ⅓ size, see page 94.)

Doll body 15¾in (40cm)

Part A: Sew the middle seam.

Part B: Sew the middle seam.

Part A and B: Place right-hand pieces on right-hand pieces and sew the side seams up to the mark .

Part C: Sew ¾in (2cm) of the thigh piece. Then place the legs right on right onto Part A and sew the side seams. Afterwards, sew the inside of the legs.

Finally, insert Part D on the back and the back of the legs.

Pattern for a Dress

(Reduced to approximately $\frac{1}{3}$ size, see pages 102 & 103.)

Material needed: $35^3/_8$in (90cm), if fabric is $55^3/_4$in (140cm) wide.
Skirt length: $17^5/_8$in (45cm) cut.
Finished length: $16^1/_2$in (42cm).

COMPLETION
Sew the back skirt seam to the opening and clean. Gather the skirt on top to measure $17^3/_8$in (44cm).

UPPER PART
Lay right side on right side. Sew shoulder seams and side seams with $7/_{16}$in (1cm) seam allowances and clean. Hem the back seam. Sew the skirt right side on right side onto the upper part and smooth.

SLEEVES
Gather the upper sleeve to about $7^1/_2$in (19cm), right side on right side; sew onto the lower sleeve. Make a hem of $7/_{16}$in as (1cm) on lower arm. Sew the side seams and smooth. Gather the upper arm and right side on right side sew into the front part. Smooth out the arm segment.

COLLAR
Lay collar right side on right side, sew edge-wise with $7/_{16}$in (1cm) seam allowance and turn. Sew the collar onto the front piece and clean it with a bias strip. Sew the bias strip onto the collar and by hand, sew it onto the inside of the dress.

Afterwards make a $7/_{16}$in (1cm) hem and place the snaps on the back seam.

Seam

leave open

Hem

Skirt

cut 1

Gather (crimp) to approx. $17^3/_8$in (44cm)

Breach

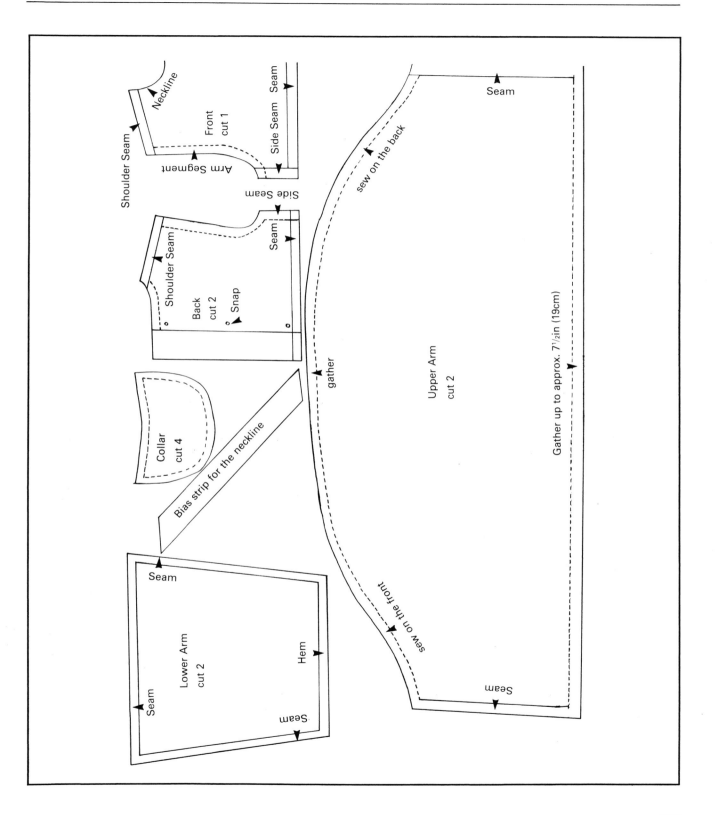

Neckline

Shoulder Seam

Front
cut 1

Arm Segment

Side Seam   Seam

Side Seam

Shoulder Seam

Back
cut 2

Snap

Seam

sew on the back

Seam

Upper Arm
cut 2

gather

Gather up to approx. 7½in (19cm)

Collar
cut 4

Bias strip for the neckline

Seam

Lower Arm
cut 2

Hem

Seam

Seam

sew on the front

Seam

*Chapter 8*_____

The Modelling And Completion Of A Portrait Head

The Three Dimensional

When making dolls, you not only have the possibility of producing your own fantasy dolls, but you can produce a copy of a living model. To achieve a relatively good result, it is necessary that your dominate your handicraft perfectly. Handicraft means to see two-dimensionally and transfrom it into three-dimensional, whereby it is necessary to put back your own artistic expression, since face and form (hands, feet, body structure) of the doll should correspond to the original. You naturally comes to lose your own artistic freedom, and that in the true sense. You do not have the freedom to model a face the way you want to, but are forced to model the face using a photograph or that of a living person. This type of modelling has very little to do with the artistic creation of my other dolls and that is why it does not appear in Chapter 2 under modelling.

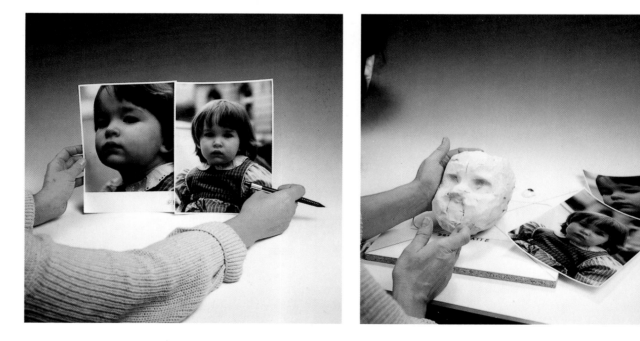

Study the photograph carefully. To make it easier, divide the photograph into squares.

First step: The rough modelling of the face.

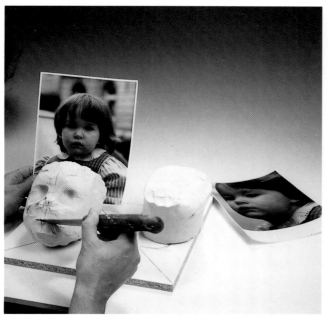

Make the proportions in the face.

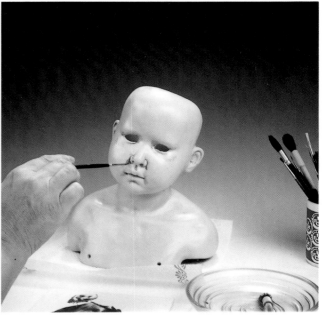

Always compare the model head with the photograph.

Head and breast plate are connected. With this type it is possible to model the shoulder bone and the neck.

The skin color is applied to the fired porcelain head.

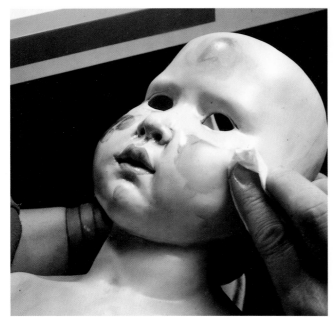

Applying the color to the cheeks and forehead.

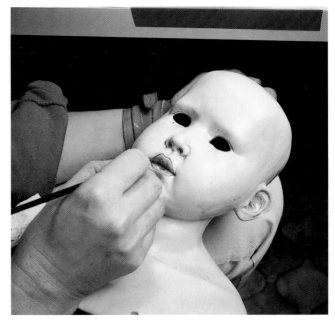

The delicate painting of the mouth.

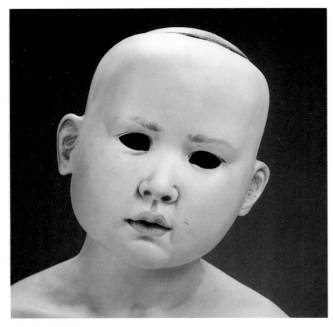

The fired and painted head.

I discovered this child among the visitors at an exhibition in the Gallery Calica in Essen.

The finished porcelain head made from a photograph. ▶

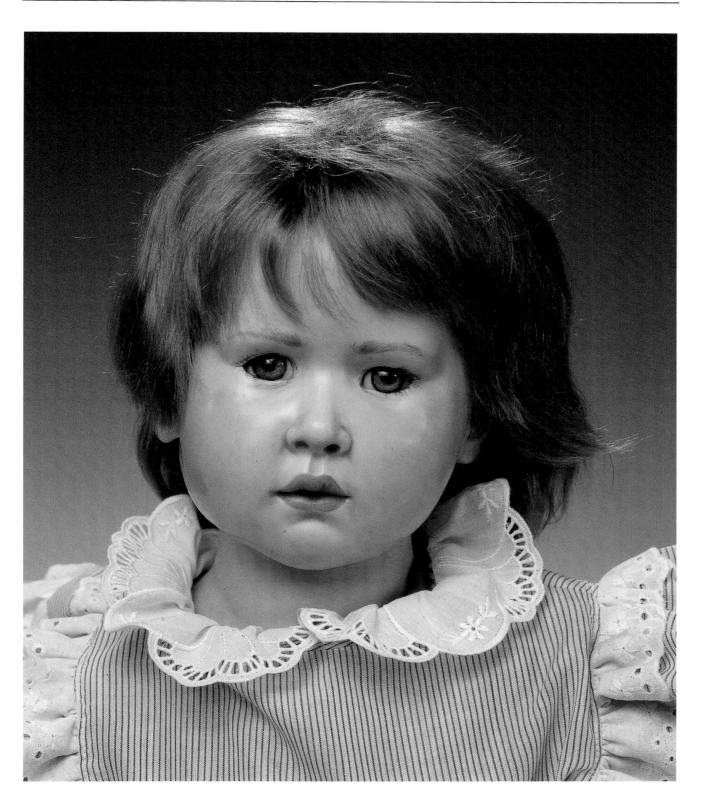

Chapter 9

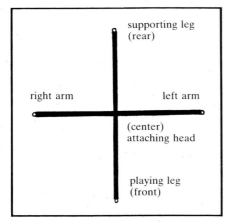

Attaching the threads to the marionette-cross.

Painting

Closed Head

Artist Doll Molds

If nothing should succeed immediately as you want it, think about the idiom "practice makes perfect." Do not despair. With perseverance, you will get nearer to your desired goal. If this path seems to be too troublesome or you are afraid to take risks to model your own artist doll and make the mold, you have the option to acquire a certain technical routine with an artist doll mold.

With the making of this doll, you can practice the casting, learn how to cut out the eyes and you can leave your fantasy roaming freely when painting. All of this you cannot do when making a reproduction.

With reproductions it is the aim of every artist that the doll should look as close as possible to the original. The painting should match with the old doll and the clothing and body must be copied from the original.

With the painting of a doll from an artist doll mold, it is not necessary that it should look like the original. The molds are made from artist dolls and are, therefore, suitable for those interested in this hobby.

To learn how to use porcelain material, I have designed a doll for beginners. It is a baby with closed eyes, the simplest type of doll for those who want to start this hobby. You can paint her according to your own desires and making the doll is rather easy. *Baby Jenny* has a dome head and flange neck which is simply tied into the body.

The next artist doll mold, after making the first doll successfully, is *Baby Nicole*. I paid special attention with the designing of both babies that the degree of difficulty from the first baby to the second one had increased so that a certain learning process would take place. *Nicole* has open eyes and the top of the head is opened. Through this opening the eyes can be inserted. The mouth of this baby is open and if you want it to be more difficult, you can insert teeth and a tongue for *Nicole*. Both are available in special hobby stores. Teeth and tongue are attached with wax. Do not forget that with *Nicole* you have cut out the eyes, mouth and the top of the head after you have casted it.

The finished doll from the mold *Baby Jenny. Photograph: H. Rochelt.*

The finished doll from the mold *Georgina.*

With a very fine brush you delicately paint the mouth. *Bajazzo* and his dancer are pictured on page 110.

The mold *Bajazzo*. The colors of the painting should be in harmony with the clothing.

◄ *Bajazzo* and his dancer. Both of these dolls are a bit unusual. The emphasis lies in the painting. A fantasy type of painting is wanted! Whether you lean towards the models of *"Comedia dell 'Arte,"* which was my original thinking or if you want to develop your own style is your decision.

Bajazzo is wearing a suit made of hand-painted silk. The costume including the hat are very similar to the classical harlequin costume.

The dancer is dancing in a fantasy dress made of silk, velvet and tulle. For details, see page 109. *Bajazzo* has won a prize at a competition of the "Gold Coast Company" in 1985 in Australia.

Index

Materials discussed in this book are available from numerous sources. Consult your favorite doll supply source. Mr. Wanke can be contacted at:

M. Wanke GmbH
Robert-Bosch-Strasse 6
D-65549 LIMBURG
Telefon: 06431/3047